W9-ACG-551

An Old Testament Study Guide

BS 1194 .B74o
ST. JOSEPH'S UNIVERSITY
STX
An Old Testament study guide,

3 9353 00005 5267

An Old Testament Study Guide

BY

MEMBERS OF THE BOSTON COLLEGE
THEOLOGY DEPARTMENT

06179

BOSTON COLLEGE PRESS
CHESTNUT HILL, MASSACHUSETTS

BS
1194
.B74 o

Copyright © 1961 by
BOSTON COLLEGE PRESS
Chestnut Hill, Massachusetts

Library of Congress Catalogue Card No.: 61-17313

NIHIL OBSTAT

Rt. Rev. Matthew P. Stapleton
Diocesan Censor

IMPRIMI POTEST

James E. Coleran, S.J.
Praep. Prov. Novae Angliae

IMPRIMATUR

Richard Cardinal Cushing
Archbishop of Boston

May 31, 1961

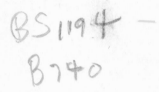

PRINTED IN THE UNITED STATES OF AMERICA

ACKNOWLEDGMENTS

The authors wish to thank Rev. Frederick L. Moriarty, S.J., of Weston College, for reading the manuscript and for his valuable advice and scholarly suggestions.

It is a special pleasure to thank M. J. C. for finding time, in a busy schedule, to do the sketch of the greatest of the prophets which appears on the cover.

Finally, we wish to thank the following publishers for their kind permission to reprint selections from their publications:

Fides, publishers of *Perspectives,* for "Bread for the Faithful" by Roderick A. F. Mackenzie, S.J., August-September, 1959. Burns, Oates and Washbourne, Ltd. for "The Value and Significance of the Old Testament" by Most Reverend Alban Goodier, S.J., from the Cambridge Catholic Summer School Studies, 1938. *The Furrow* for "The Bible in Perspective," by James Brennan, Volume 8, no. 11, December 1957, and for "The World of the Bible," by Donal O'Connor, Volume 8, no. 3, March 1957. *The Catholic Biblical Quarterly* for "Before Abraham Was . . ." by Roderick A. F. Mackenzie, S.J., Volume XV, 1953, and the text of the translation of the reply of the Biblical Commission to Cardinal Suhard, Volume X, 1948. The Catholic Truth Society of London for its complete translation of *Divino Afflante Spiritu.* The Princeton University Press for *Ancient Near Eastern Texts* by J. B. Pritchard, Ed., copyrighted 1950, 1955. B. Herder Book Co. of St. Louis for the excerpt of *"Humani Generis"* from *The Church Teaches,* 1955. The Weston College Press for the Glossary and Guide to Pronunciation from *Foreword to the Old Testament* by Frederick L. Moriarty, S.J., 1954.

FOREWORD

The purpose of this book, as indicated by its title, is to help students understand and appreciate the Old Testament. The material here compiled is the result of the Old Testament course taught at Boston College. This course was begun under Rev. William V. E. Casey, S.J., and Rev. William Leonard, S.J., in the early 1950's. After a period of time, it was clear that the Department needed a text which would outline the subject matter of an assignment, indicate what was important, and so structure the material that the student might have the direction necessary for intelligent study.

The questions have been so arranged that each set contains the matter sufficient for a class hour's instruction. The professor can use them as the basis of classroom discussion, as an outline for his lecture, or finally, adapt them to the background and ability of his students.

The professors who have worked on this Study Guide are: Rev. David F. Carroll, S.J., Rev. James J. Casey, S.J., Rev. Joseph Connor, S.J., Rev. J. Frank Devine, S.J., Rev. Joseph F. Donahue, S.J., Rev. Jeremiah J. Donovan, S.J., and Rev. Richard W. Rousseau, S.J.

TABLE OF CONTENTS

PART I

Background and Collateral Material

B.

PART II

Questions on the Individual Books
of the Old Testament

PART III

APPENDICES

PART 1

Background and Collateral Material

CHAPTER I

Bread for the Faithful[1]

R. A. F. MACKENZIE, S.J.

It is a privilege for me to participate in the important work that you envisage in this institute, that of communicating to the grade school, high school, and college levels of education that great development and flowering of theology which exists in the Church today. So far, this has been seeping down only in trickles from the higher levels of the dogmatic theologian, professional liturgist, and so on. However, in view of the great importance it has, the possibilities that it opens up for catechetical work at all levels, it is by all means desirable that we should hasten the diffusion of modern twentieth-century theological knowledge to all the faithful in the Church. This bread should be broken for the little ones, and in those "little ones" we can include all those who come to us to acquire an education in Catholic schools.

My purpose here will not be to draw pedagogical conclusions; that I leave to you. Remaining rather in my own particular field, I will attempt to give some survey of the situation in Scripture studies as they exist at present in the Catholic Church. Many of you, perhaps all of you, are aware that there is here a very great treasure of truth and

---

[1] In chapters I-V a few minor changes have been made. To aid the student, the spellings of certain words have been standardized. It also seemed advisable to alter some dates given in the original articles.

insight which needs to be more widespread and more generally communicated. Much of what I will say will not be
new to many of you; but putting it together and presenting it on one occasion in a general survey may provide a
useful basis for more detailed discussion and application.

I will divide my matter under three headings, three general aspects of Scripture studies. The first one will be the
background of the Bible, the greatly improved knowledge
that we have nowadays of the civilization, the culture, the
general human condition against which the books of the
Bible must be situated. The second topic is the literary
aspect, or, let us say, the *improved literary understanding*
of the formation of the books of the Bible—the much
better insight we have today into the process by which these
books were actually written by human authors. The third
topic is that to which the other two are meant to lead, and
to which in fact they have led; it is the product of those
two factors. I mean our advance in *religious understanding of the Bible,* both Old and New Testaments. We can
now have a certain grasp of the message of the two Testaments such as was, humanly speaking, not really possible
a hundred years ago. Actually, it was not really prevalent
even twenty years ago. This deeper religious understanding
has developed, somewhat paradoxically, from our deeper
penetration into the human background and human origins of the Bible.

Background of the Bible

Let us begin, then, with our concrete knowledge of the
background of the Bible. A hundred years ago, if a Bible
history had to be written, especially in the sense of a history of the Old Testament, it was quite narrowly limited
to interpretation of the data provided by the sacred books
themselves. There was scarcely anything in the way of

comparison, of outside checking, of other sources of information, by which the process of the history of the people of Israel could be situated against a larger background. Certainly, it was located against the general history of humanity in the period in which it took place. However, until one came down to the history of Greece, let us say, beginning about the sixth century, B.C., there was really very little comparative material against which to set off the historical narration of the Bible. Even the Greek, Hellenistic, or Roman background was in its details considerably less fully known than it is today.

A most noticeable contrast to this picture has developed in the past hundred years. We have now a quite detailed, satisfactorily full and clear history of the Near East in what archaeologists call the Middle and Late Bronze Ages and the Iron Age, roughly the second and first millennia B.C. It is this Near East that is the geographical theater of the history of Israel. We have a knowledge of the politics, of the successive reigns of kings, the campaigns, the wars, the rising of one nation and the fall of another, comparable to our knowledge, let us say, of sections of European history in the Christian era. The history of the Dark Ages in Europe, sixth to tenth centuries A.D., is not much better known to us than is the history of the Assyrian kingdom in the tenth to the seventh centuries B.C. That makes for a vastly improved concretization of our knowledge of the history of Israel.

As a result, the picture presented in the book of Exodus, or in the books of Kings, is no longer a sort of fairy-book picture of events taking place in a "never-never land," something outside of the world of space and time which we know, but something that we can pin down and insert and locate accurately and satisfactorily on a broader canvas, against the broader picture of human development and human history. Immediately, therefore, we have a better contact with, a sense of the immediacy of, sacred history itself.

Most of the increase of knowledge I am speaking of stems directly or indirectly from the science of archaeology, from the actual physical excavation of the remains of those ancient peoples, the careful uncovering of different strata on sites of ancient Eastern cities. It is revealed to us either immediately through the architecture, through the building plans, through the material remains found, or else mediately through the literature thus recovered. All this information about those ancient civilizations, from Egypt eastward through the land of Canaan and Syria to the northern part of Mesopotamia, down through Mesopotamia itself to the eastern end of the Fertile Crescent, still in the East in Elam, on the north in Armenia, then westward through what is now Asia Minor, the Aegean area, and the western portions of the Mediterranean basin—all this information has been gathered by archaeologists.

Patiently excavating many hundreds of sites, they have pieced together the evidence from these sites themselves, and by comparisons they have arrived at this enormous development of ancient history of which we have spoken. We know, for example, the development of the New Kingdom in Egypt, the glorious and high civilization of the Pharaohs; we know of the Hyksos invading Egypt in the first half of the second millennium B.C., and the high international civilization that reigned in the Middle Bronze Age; and we know of the Hittite kingdom, totally unknown sixty years ago, ruling from the central area of what is now Turkey. We know of the kingdom of the Mitannians on the upper Euphrates in the fourteenth and thirteenth centuries B.C. We know also of the first dynasty of Babylon; and, coming down into the first millennium, the great and flourishing development of the Assyrian Empire, the first real world empire (as the world was then known); the break-up and collapse of that empire at the hands of the Medes and Persians, its disruption at the overwhelming advance of Alexander; the irruption of Greece into the world of the Near East, the Hellenistic Age marked by that tremendous flowering of Greek civilization throughout the countries bordering on the eastern Mediterranean. Then the steady penetration eastward of Rome, the power that enveloped the civil frontier province of Palestine, of Judea, and, through mismanagement and oppression, that led in the year 68 A.D. to the explosion which was the final Jewish revolt, terminating in the destruction of the nation with all its sacred places and Temple in the year 70 A.D.

All that history gives us a magnificent sweep and is in itself, of course, a very valuable and precious extension of human knowledge into the things of the past. However, from our present point of view, it is vastly more precious, because against that great sweep of international history we can now situate the development, the experiences, the travails, the reactions, the positive errors, the repeated falls and repeated returns to their God of the nation of Israel— a history in itself more appealing, more mysterious, more fascinating than the history of any of the other nations, and, to the eyes of faith, a marvelous example of the patient education by God of His chosen human creatures. The experience of Israel, of which I will speak, is the experience of all of us in a sense: there is a vocation; there is a response to the vocation; there is infidelity; and there are repeated calls by God; and, let us hope, in the case of Israel, as in our individual cases, there is a happy ending, a final reconciliation and final rejoicing.

We can fill out that outline of history now because of our better knowledge of the *thought-world* that went with it. By that I mean the ideas, the culture, the outlook on life, the customs and conventions, all the group psychology of those mysterious peoples, both Semitic and non-Semitic, who inhabited those lands and who experienced that tumultuous and complex history. Here we come still closer to the history of the people of God: the rest of the history of which we have spoken is only a background; the history of Babylon is not the history of Israel. But the thought-world of Babylon is in part the thought-world of Israel; and therefore it is of great importance to the student of the Old Testament who wishes to penetrate the ways of thinking, the presuppositions, the conventions of language, the things taken for granted by the chroniclers and prophets and wise men of Israel. To do this, he must understand them against the setting of the presuppositions, etc., of the wise men of Babylonia, of Syria, of Egypt, perhaps most of all of Canaan.

Fortunately, as we said, archaeologists have uncovered not merely the physical remains, the artifacts, the construction of buildings, fortifications and weapons, and so on. They have rediscovered for us and deciphered the literatures of those peoples, the literature of ancient Egypt, the literature of Babylonia, the literature of Canaan, a large representation of the literature of the Hittites, and many partial and fragmentary remains of other peoples like the Mitannians. All that is immensely precious because it gives a direct insight from contemporary documents into the way those people lived and thought and worked and conceived their world. Their myths, their accounts as to how the gods originated, how the gods worked, how the gods created this world, how the gods created man—all of these have a certain bearing on corresponding accounts in the Old Testament. Their technique of chronicle writing, their selectiveness, their organization of the records of their own past, have close connections with the oldest historical forms of writing in the Old Testament. Their omen literature, that is to say, their oracles given to guide men in their future behavior, lucky and unlucky days, lucky and unlucky behavior, how to ensnare the good will of their gods and how to avoid their curse, has certain parallels in the prophetic literature of Israel. More than that, there have been found, at Mari on the middle Euphrates, reports from soothsayers (dating from about the seventeenth century B.C.) which are strikingly similar in style to some of the oracles of the prophets of Israel. Later I will come to speak about the distinctive and unique marks of Israelite civilization, but right now I am emphasizing the resemblances. We see, for example, that the oracle style "Thus said Yahweh . . ." is not specific to Israel except for the name of the god for whom it is used. Again, the rituals, the liturgy, the cult, the organization of worship offered by these peoples to their gods are parallel to the ritual and cult of Israel, and in many cases they preceded the cult of Israel.

Much else could be added in connection with their law codes, the position of the king, their civilization, and so on. For the moment, let us speak only of the literary connections. A great deal of light has been shed, particularly on the forms of literature, by finding the origins of ancestors or parallels of Israelite forms in the early Near-Eastern literature. More than that, more than just the literature, the religion itself of Israel is greatly illuminated by that Eastern background. In their worship of this strange, unique God who had called them through Moses, the Israelites spontaneously and naturally adopted the whole vocabulary, the whole complexus of rites, actions, and techniques by which the gods of that area and that age were worshipped. There is animal sacrifice; there is sacred dance and procession; there is the composition of sacred song, psalms of lament, of petition, of glorification, of expiation, of cursing, and so on. The concept of a special sacred place or of a temple is not something original with Israel; and, as we well know, the concept of priesthood was taken over from other peoples by Israel. One can go through most of the external forms of religion in Israel and show that they have analogues in those other religions; therefore there existed between Israel and those other religions a certain likeness of mentality. For that reason, we understand Israel better by seeing how those other peoples conceived their forms of worship, what they thought they accomplished by them, what they intended them to be.

Other points of similarity exist in the areas of sociology and law. There are parallels to the tribal system of Israel, this strange religious federation of originally separate tribes who were united simply by their service of one unique god, whose connection was primarily religious, whose social unity consisted precisely in meeting periodically at a given place of worship to renew collectively their allegiance to their god. The Israelite idea of family organization, the subordination of the individual to the head of the family, the real "survival" of the family head in his descendents—all these are part of the common thought-world of the Near East. Common to Israel and to her neighbors is the idea of salvation, what they expected from their god. The semi-nomadic condition of the people at the time of Moses, their gradual transition to sedentary living, the movement from simple encampment to village life and then to life in towns, the transition of a good portion of the people to commercial practice, to the middle-man status, instead of their previous life as simple herdsmen— this is all vividly reflected in the books of the Old Testament, in the images used, in the forms in which God presented Himself to the people, in their experiences; and all those factors are better understood by us in proportion as we understand the ancient Eastern sociology.

The position of the king in Israelite society as seen by the group of prophets around David is the foundation for the doctrine of royal messianism, which becomes so important in later Jewish thinking; and its importance extends into the New Testament, especially in St. John's Gospel, and has remained in the Church. The figure of the king behind this messianism depends ultimately upon the Near Eastern concept of the king as we find it in the second millennium B.C. We notice, in the Bible, how important it was for the Israelites of the eleventh century B.C. to have a king. The king was himself the representative of the whole people, in a sense so real that we can hardly grasp it. He summed up the people; what happened to him happened to them; bad luck befalling him, bad health, weakness, affected everyone else in the commonwealth. And if the king became incompetent and helpless in the performance of his duties he must be removed and another more effective substituted. It was not a matter of punishment or vengeance; it was simply a matter of public safety.

It was only after a period of struggle that the king took such a place of importance in Israel, because within the Israelite commonwealth the king could not be the religious figure he was in other countries. He was not provided for in the charter of Mosaic religion, and hence there is an ambiguous and two-sided attitude towards the kingship. The king was necessary, and yet he was an intruder; this was a problem that Israel never really solved. Eventually, the kingship was abandoned and Israel continued its life, but in the four centuries when the kingship was used by them it gave origin to that tremendous doctrine of messianism.

Just as comparative studies draw our attention to the

importance attached to the figure of the king, so, too, they have high-lighted the importance of the law. As we know, there were many ancient codes of law: the famous code of Hammurabi, the Assyrian codes of the fourteenth century B.C., the laws of the Hittites, as well as the pre-Hammurabi codes. All of these throw light on the pride of the Israelites in the possession of their own code of laws. One of the greatest benefits that Yahweh had given the Israelites in their Exodus from Egypt and the revelation at Sinai was His granting to them a constitution of their own. He had created Israel, He had made them into a people, He had formed them into a united society, and to mark that action He had granted to them a code of laws. Law is not seen as something restrictive; it is a great boon, a blessing. Their law makes them grow up, permits them to hold up their heads among the other societies of the time.

Again, the fact and the idea of a covenant, so central to the Old Testament, are greatly clarified by recent investigations of Hittite covenant treaties. Even more than the idea of royalty, the idea of covenant is important as a theme in the Old Testament. Actually, it corresponds to the Church's doctrine of sanctifying grace, of supernatural love. It was under that formality that the special supernatural relationship of men to God was presented to this chosen people called out of Egypt: namely, an arbitrary, freely-chosen, freely-willed adoption of these people, a raising of them into a special friendship with God. Yet, the idea of covenant, chosen to embody the tremendous concept and truth of grace, was drawn from the sociological situation of the times, modeled upon the action of the Hittite kings, in particular, in making covenants with subordinate princes and with their vassals. Covenant was a freely-bestowed relationship that established a certain bond between the great king and his subordinates, a bond based upon his beneficence towards them. In gratitude for that, the subordinate is bound to be loyal always to the great king, never to deal with his enemies, never to rebel against him, to pay him regular tribute, and to acknowledge no other overlord. To match these fourteenth century treaties with the provisions of the Mosaic covenant which date from the thirteenth century, throws a great deal of light on the understanding the Israelites had of this latter.

Literary Origins of the Bible

My second main area of discussion is that of the literary origins, or rather the better understanding we now possess regarding the literary forms and the origins of the Old Testament books. If you are familiar with the encyclical *Divino Afflante Spiritu* of fifteen years ago (on the progress of biblical studies), you will know that one of the things stressed in that encyclical is the analysis of the literary forms of different sections of the Old and New Testaments. Such analysis, says the Pope equivalently, is the key to our correct understanding of what the human authors, and through them the divine author, are trying to say. The great advance of non-Catholic scholars and of Catholic scholars, too, in this literary analysis is one of the outstanding characteristics of the modern biblical revival. Of our two great sources, or criteria, for determining and interpreting these *genera literaria* (literary forms), one is external: the comparison with the other literatures of which I have just spoken. The other is internal: from literary analysis itself, from the techniques of determining an author's meaning from the context, from the whole bearing of his writing.

We have come to see very clearly that we are dealing with literary forms that are specific to those periods of the world's history, specific to those cultures and civilizations.

They are in great part more or less alien to our contemporary ideas; alien, that is, to the literary forms used by us today, classified by our librarians, represented in our newspapers or in the books we read. Of our forms, none quite correspond to any one of the biblical forms, and, on the other hand, no one of the biblical forms perfectly corresponds to a form that we use today. Those forms of writing are fixed, conventional means of expression. The author who wanted to convey, let us say, the truth of something that happened in the past, had a set and conventional way of doing so, a set stock of expressions to indicate what he was talking about, a set stock of images, of constructions, of symbols, by which to convey his meaning.

Let us just take the wisdom literature as an example. Many important parts of the Old Testament are wisdom literature: the book of Proverbs, Qoheleth, the book of Job, Ben Sira, many of the Psalms, the book of Baruch (at least in part), and some other smaller sections. Such wisdom literature is a highly developed genre in the literature of the ancient Near East. In these writings we find a conventionalized attribution of such wisdom to the ruler; so also among the Jews: the regular expression for any wisdom writing is "book of Solomon," because the convention was to put such wisdom writing in the mouth of a former king. Wisdom was part of God's gift to the king, and therefore the king was the final exponent of wisdom. Such conventional usages no more deceived or bothered readers of those days than do our modern conventions of novel writing, for example, our "historical fiction" written in the first person.

We have already spoken of parallels to many of the kinds of Psalms and of the similarity of prophetic oracles within and outside the Israelite people. Now I can mention briefly the question that is perhaps most interesting in this regard: the possibility—and for present-day scholarship it is a certainty—that there are different literary genres within the historical writings of the Bible. For some sixty years or so this has been the subject of quite strenuous, and at times bitter, controversy in the Church. Today, it is peaceably settled and agreed upon; but the specific applications to be drawn from these literary insights are still being worked out.

One of these points is, that not all narrative is *ipso facto* historic. I hope that that sounds perfectly obvious, but you would be surprised to find how often in older books *truthful* and *historical* are equated; if a thing isn't historical, it isn't true. Probably the best starting point in discussing this matter is a consideration of the parables of the Gospels. We all know that the parables are stories related by Our Lord. They are fiction; they never happened. And if Our Lord could use that form of literature, why could not the authors of the Old Testament do so? —as some of them, in fact, did.

Even here it is helpful to distinguish two types of parables. There is a type of parable that is completely timeless, and there is a type that is historical in a certain way, in that it treats of God's dealings with Israel. An example of the first type is the parable of the Prodigal Son; its teaching is the truth of the mercy of God. This parable is most unfortunately named: the central figure is really the father, and the parable would be better called the parable of the Loving Father. However, my principal point in its regard is that this parable is not a presentation of one instance in history or one historical period or situation rather than another.

On the other hand, consider the parable of the unjust caretakers of the vineyard, the parable of those left in charge of the vineyard, to whom the owner sent messengers to collect the rent, and who, refusing to pay the rent, reject and punish these messengers. Finally the owner sends his own son; he is not only rejected but killed by the caretakers. That parable really is an historical parable, because under the symbol of the vineyard, of the rent, of the landowner and tenants, you have symbolized the history of the Jewish people up to and including the time of Christ. It is symbolic history.

Besides parables, there are, of course, many other genera, many other literary forms; these require their own kind of interpretation, often quite different from that to which we are accustomed. There are chronicles and genealogies, lists of names and places, legends of ancient heroes, sagas about the history of ancient peoples; and for all of these one can find parallels in the other ancient literatures of which I have spoken. One of the most interesting of these parallels is that of the type we might call edifying or religious fiction; this we can find, for example, in Egypt, and in biblical books like Jonah or Tobit. In all such writings, when we wish to interpret them, it is the intention of the human author that is of primary importance. We must not treat such books as if they had been written by our contemporaries; we must not assume that a biblical author means by his writings what we would have meant in writing them today. We must ask what the author meant *then*, what he intended to convey.

A parallel that I sometimes find helpful, in explaining this to people who raise the question of the degree of historicity in Old Testament narrative, is that of Shakespeare's plays. There is, first of all, the distinction between Shakespeare's tragedies and his histories. As an example of the first, take *King Lear*. I have no doubt that there was some ancient legend from early British history which concerned a King Lear who was badly treated by his daughters; but Shakespeare in writing his play is not the least bit concerned about the historicity of this man's existence or the reality of his daughters. All he is concerned about is the use he can make of this in writing a play; he has taken the name and possibly the outline of the plot from a dubiously historical story. This might be paralleled to something like the book of Job. There is no sense in wasting time or breath in discussing whether there ever was an historical Job; we have no idea, and it is extremely unimportant. What is important in the book of Job is what the author does with his hero, his Job.

Take another Shakespearean play, *Hamlet*, or *Macbeth*. There was a king named Macbeth; if I am not mistaken, he lived in the eleventh century, killed his predecessor, and was killed by his predecessor's son. To that extent, the play gives an outline of genuine Scottish history. Yet, even here, where Shakespeare has taken his story of Macbeth from history, it is what Shakespeare has made of Macbeth that is important. It would be ridiculous if one writing Scottish history should say "Fortunately, we have full information about Macbeth and his queen, because Shakespeare wrote a play about them." No, the Macbeth in his play is Shakespeare's creation. There is an historical nucleus to the play, if you wish, but Shakespeare has used it only to present one of his wonderful studies of human nature, of guilt, temptation, and tragedy.

We can come, then, to a third form: Shakespeare's histories, his chronicle plays—*Richard II, Richard III, Henry IV, Henry V*, etc. First of all, the events in these plays are closer in time to the Elizabethan period; Shakespeare has taken them mainly from Holinshed's *Chronicles*, a fairly detailed book of history; and he is at pains to preserve in general, and even in some particulars, the original history.

But he still has added a great deal of his own to the story. There is something analogous to these differing levels of historicity in Shakespeare in the Bible—for example, the books of Samuel might correspond somewhat to the last-named type of Shakespearean usage of history. However, I would not want to stress these comparisons too much, because Shakespeare's plays are still non-Hebraic in literary form.

Much more could be said about literary forms in the Bible; we might add just a word about the New Testament. In the New Testament we are not helped by comparison with other literatures as we are with regard to the Old. The New Testament is unique, even in a literary way, in its literary form, to an extent that the Old is not. But this much at least we can say: there has been a tendency to impose upon the Gospels a historicity which their authors did not aim or care about. Most of the lives of Christ written in the last hundred years or so have tended to impose such historicity; for example, to try to work out a strict sequence of events in Christ's public life, for which we have no real basis. The Gospels are recordings of the preaching of the early Church at a time when the original generation of witnesses began to die out, thirty, forty, or fifty years after the events of Christ's life. They record, therefore, in fixed form, with a certain leeway left to each Evangelist, already determined groups and sequences of teachings about the birth, earthly life, and death of Our Lord. One can see the general outline of this early teaching in each of the Gospel narratives: Baptism, public life, Passion and Resurrection accounts. That is the framework common to all the Gospels; but within this framework the different Evangelists enjoyed great freedom, and they have grouped their matter according to certain pedagogical intentions of their own. Matthew, Mark, Luke, and John arranged their matter, not because this event came after that event, rather than before it, but because this sequence served the pedagogical intentions of which we just spoke.

Although the Gospels are definitely historical, they are historical in this particular way; and they do not have the concern about chronological sequence that we would expect in modern biography. Actually, they are not biographies; in the true sense it is impossible to try to write the life of Our Lord, and the Evangelists did not attempt it. What they did attempt to convey was a better understanding of the work of Christ, and this for Christians who already believed.

Religious Understanding of the Bible

Now, somewhat belatedly, I come to my third point: the improved religious understanding of the Bible. This, of course, is that toward which the previous two aspects of biblical studies are aimed, for it gives them their importance and meaning. In *Divino Afflante Spiritu*, the Pope speaks of our first point, improved knowledge of the background and setting of the Bible, as something already quite well achieved. The second point, study of the Bible according to its different literary forms, is something that the Pope recommends—one might almost say imposes—as something necessary and urgent in the work of the exegete. This third point, improved religious understanding of the Bible, is rather a pious hope to which the Pope looks forward. He expresses his confidence that this will be the result of the other two; and we may say that within the last fifteen years the Pope's expectation has been most consolingly fulfilled. The flood of writings on the Bible among European Catholics, especially in the last fifteen years, has been concerned very largely with the exploitation of its religious values, as we can see them and apply them to ourselves.

There is no longer question merely of picking out separate or isolated stories from the Bible, and drawing moralistic lessons from them of virtues to be practiced and vices to be avoided. Nor is there question of isolating texts, to be interpreted as one would interpret a definition by a Church Council or a sentence from Canon Law. That tended to be the treatment a hundred years ago, the treatment of the Old Testament in our Bible History books, a chopped-up treatment that did not seem to value the Old Testament for its own sake. Now, in our modern approach, Christ is the center of the Old Testament, just as He is of the New. The message of the two parts in the Bible is one, and the Old Testament by itself is a magnificent testimony to the one salvation history. The Old Testament is not primarily a history of Israel or of human events as such; it is a history of God. It is a history of the things that God has worked through and in Israel, recorded by witnesses, testified to by the collective experience of the people, transmitted to posterity precisely because such is the duty and obligation of the sacred writers—a history that possesses from beginning to end, despite all the varieties of expression and differences of outlook and of thought, a unity that is unmistakable, a unity that is due, not to human psychology or to human authorship, but to the action of God which is recorded in the Bible. For that reason, the salvation history is one story from beginning to end.

The history of Israel as such begins only with the book of Exodus, with the constitution of the people of God out of a group of fugitives from Egypt, to whom God had sent the one man Moses. Israel as a people did not exist until they had crossed the Red Sea and begun their wandering in the desert. But from that point, the salvation history, with the great destiny attributed to this people, follows its course for centuries. All the prophets, all the wise men, all the chroniclers and historians of Israel deal with that one situation, with that one theme; what God intends to make of Israel and the difficult time He has in accomplishing this. The literature of Israel is an extraordinary example of national humility—one of the many ways in which it is unique. I know of absolutely no other national literature in the world's history in which the nation is not glorified; the theme of Israel's literature is that of Psalm 113—"Non nobis, Domine, non nobis, sed nomini tuo da gloriam." It is Yahweh, their God, whom their literature intends to glorify from beginning to end. With astounding humility, Israel makes of its own history one long act of self-accusation and of contrition.

Thus, the Old Testament, just as the New, is testimony to a connected history of God; and that connected history is the working out in practice of what God is: a salvation God, a Being of overwhelming goodness who intends to have mankind with Him for eternity, who wishes them to be happy, who offers them salvation such as no earthly power can offer. These stories of the Old Testament can stand in their own right as the history of Israel, but actually they are part of a pulsating divine activity that is repeated again and again in history. Here it is that we come to that great connection between the Old and the New Testament of which the Fathers of the Church made so much, which they saw so clearly. This connection has always been preserved in the Church's liturgy, but it has not been much exploited until very recent times. What I am referring to is what is known as typology, by which I mean the expressly willed similarity between the way God treated

Israel and Israel responded to God, and the way God the Father dealt with Christ and Christ's response to His Father. To carry it still further, there is the similarity between the way the Father dealt with Christ and the way God deals with the members of the Church.

This typology, on which patristic literature laid so much stress, is obviously of great catechetical importance. In the early Church, as we know, before the theology of the sacraments was elaborated speculatively as it came to be by the late Middle Ages, the meaning of the sacraments was largely explained to the people in terms of typology. If you want to know what that typology was—let us say of Baptism—read the early chapters of Exodus and see what happens in the "baptism" of the Israelites: how they were led through water and delivered from the servitude of a pagan power, led from an anti-god power into the service of God. So, too, in Baptism: the passing down into the baptismal font and coming out of the water was to the early Christians a symbolic re-enactment of the passage of the Israelites through the Red Sea. It was a similar salvation of God effected upon them and effected upon Israel, with the difference that this Christian salvation is a salvation through Christ and into Christ; nevertheless there was the fundamental sameness of Exodus and Baptism. Again, with respect to the Eucharist, the figure of the manna in the desert was a particularly favored reference in the early Church; the Eucharist is the support and nourishment provided by God to His people during their pilgrimage through the desert of this world, heavenly food, bread of angels, containing virtue and power and energy that no earthly food could possess; a food, therefore, to be received with utmost reverence, utmost purity, utmost gratitude by God's people. So with the other sacraments; they were explained and interpreted in terms of that typology.

While the typology meaning is secondary and dependent upon the literal historical meaning of an Old Testament passage, it is very important in making the bridge between the Old Testament and ourselves. So, too, is the prophetic role of the Old Testament, which has come to be much better understood. I mentioned earlier the rather unfortunate treatment of the messianic prophecies, by which they are pulled out of their contexts and used as isolated sentences, as examples of God in the Old Testament giving a detailed prophecy about Christ. That is not false, of course, but it is very incomplete, and easily gives a false idea; it prevents us from understanding the full richness, the true development of God's message to His people. In dealing with a prophecy, such as that of the virgin bearing a child whose name shall be called Emmanuel, we must not only ask ourselves how this finds its meaning and fulfillment when the Messiah finally comes, but we must also ask what this prophecy meant to Isaiah and to his contemporaries. It was spoken on a given day about the year 735 B.C., before a given audience that we know quite well. What did these words mean to Isaiah and to his hearers? They had some meaning then, some contemporary reference, which it is worth our while to learn.

Just a few words on the new religious understanding of the New Testament. This lags somewhat behind the development relative to the Old Testament, perhaps because there has been more need for correction in our ideas of the Old Testament. However, there has been some very stimulating and helpful work done on the analysis of New Testament literature. The key book in this recent study is the Acts of the Apostles. Starting from that book rather than from any of the Gospels, a new understanding of the genesis of the Gospels themselves has been given us.

In the first part of the Acts of the Apostles, particularly

if we combine what we find there with certain scraps from the Pauline Epistles and from some outside sources, we find an extraordinarily vivid picture of the very first period of the Church. We see the first existence of the Church, the tremendous ferment, the quickening enlightment that took place in the short span of years from about 30 to 70 A.D. We see the problem arising of finding the relationship of Christianity to Judaism, the need of working out the implications of the tremendous revolution caused by the reception into the Church of Gentile converts, who are not Jews and are not required to become Jewish proselytes before becoming Christians. And in connection with this question of the relation of Jew and Gentile in the Church, we can see the question of central authority in the Church and how it was to be administered. All these events come to life as we read the Acts of the Apostles.

When we turn from Acts to the Gospels, we see these documents as testimony to the faith of the Church in those early years. There was an interval, roughly equivalent to a man's active lifetime—about thirty or forty years—when the Church lived solely by its oral teaching (and the text of the Old Testament). Not only the preaching to unbelievers who were to be converted, but also the instruction of the catechumens and adult converts was all done orally, in the form of accounts of the life and work, the death and resurrection of Christ. Only toward the end of this period did the Gospels come to be written, when the original eye-witnesses were dying off and it became time to recall and record this oral catechesis as closely as possible in its original form. This gave rise to that fourfold presentation, in which a fixed division of the material is discernible; yet within that division great personal freedom and initiative are used by each Evangelist.

As we know from ordinary experience, a witness tells

us what he remembers, and as he remembers it, and we expect even the most faithful witnesses to any one event to give somewhat varying accounts of that event. They have seen it from different angles, have experienced it differently; one will lay more stress on this aspect, another on that. The more such witnesses we have, the better picture we can form of the actual event. Now, in this sense it is true to say that we reach Christ in the Gospels only *through* the faith of the early Church, through the faith of Matthew, Mark, Luke, and John. One runs into opposition to such a statement from people who insist that this does not satisfy them; they want to feel that when they pick up their New Testament they are in immediate contact with Christ Himself, without human intermediary, as it were; that what they see on the pages are the very words Christ spoke. However, it simply is not possible to bypass the very channel of communication that He Himself has chosen—in this case, the faith-illuminated minds of the Evangelists. With all due respect to the people mentioned, their attitude reflects an undervaluing of the incarnational aspect of Christ's revelation, a lack of understanding of the implications of the Incarnation itself, of the fact that Christ chooses to reveal Himself and speak to us through and by means of our fellow-men.

Obviously, one does not have to stress this last point with regard to the Church, Christ's own Body. What I would like to stress is that it is true also in the Church's documents: the record we have of Christ speaking. All they tell us is true, and worthy of divine faith; but, nevertheless, Christ's teaching comes to us through their instrumentality. There are innumerable instances we might cite. For example, St. John, in the great farewell discourse (John 13-18), has obviously included much material that historically must have been communicated by Our Lord after the

Resurrection. Again, the missionary discourse in Matthew 10 has two distinct parts: the first refers to the 72 disciples being sent out at that time, during the public life of Our Lord; but the second (from verse 16 on) does not fit into that situation at all—it refers to the experience of the Church after Pentecost. St. Matthew has chosen to add to the record of the original instruction a passage *which expresses Our Lord's will and teaching* for the contemporary Church. Other examples could be given. But the point I wish to make is simply this: that in order to understand the Gospels properly, to take out of them what God wishes us to find there, we must not leave out of account the human authorship, the genuine human activity that entered into their production.

CHAPTER II

The Value and Significance
of the Old Testament

Most Reverend Alban Goodier, S.J.

To realize the value and significance of the Old Testament we must begin at the very beginning. Let us suppose an open-minded student of literature who is neither a Christian nor a Jew, taking up the Old Testament for the first time. We will suppose he has studied other ancient literatures of other races, and now he wants to study the literature of the ancient Hebrews. He would find it a collection of books covering a period of much more than a thousand years. He would find it to consist of books of archaeology and history, poetry and romance, political and moral guidance, written at different times, and under different circumstances. During those thousand years and more, the people for whom and by whom these books had been written had passed through different periods of civilization, from the nomad state to that of the settled town-dweller. They had endured every vicissitude; they had been enslaved and had enjoyed the height of prosperity; they had been corrupted by internal schism and rivalry, and by the grossest forms of idolatry; they had been driven into exile far away from their own country; they had endured more than one foreign yoke; they had lost the use of their own language, which is the last thing a conquered race surrenders; they had gone through trials which would have brought absolute extinction to any ordinary people. All this the student would discover in these books; and yet, in spite of the difference of civilization which they described and in spite of all these vicissitudes, he would find in them a most astonishing unity. So much would this same tone and outlook seem to run through them all that he would come almost to disregard the dates at which the different books were written; he would find it easier to look on them as one book rather than as many.

When he studies the content of these books more closely, he will find them a record of a single people, strangely and uniquely conscious of themselves from the very beginning to the very end. Long before they have established themselves in the world, they speak of themselves as a chosen people; when they have been almost crushed out of existence, they still say the same. And this in spite of the somewhat sorry tale they have to tell of themselves. The records of other nations invariably dwell on their glories and great achievements; this record dwells rather on its people's failures and shame, and yet it never loses its consciousness of, and its confidence in, its singular greatness. It is the record of the people of God, the sons of Abraham, the children of Israel, the Kingdom of David, the observers of the Law the worshippers at one Temple. Whatever their upheavals, and wherever they have been compelled to live, they have been convinced that they are a specially-chosen people, with a special mission to fulfill, and these books are the record of the fact. They call themselves the elect of the one, true God, specially chosen by Him to represent Him in the world; and they believe that, in some way, upon them depends the salvation and the prosperity of the whole human race in the future. Hence there is another thing which the non-believing student will discover in these books, which he will find nowhere else in the literature of any other nation. Other nations describe their own attainments, their actual prowess and glory; these books describe a people who seem to live, not so much in their own generation as in the time to come; all their present achievements are but a shadow of what will some day be. They describe a prophetic people. If they would be faithful, their posterity would be multiplied as the sands of the seashore; if they observed the Law, their kingdom would come to include the whole world. From them would be born a King whom all the nations would serve, a Prophet whose law all would accept, a Priest whose sacrifice would be offered from the rising of the sun to its going down.

When next our student comes to examine the literature itself and the spirit which creates it, he will find again a marked difference between it and the literature of any other nation. All other literatures, of East or West, ancient or modern, begin with and rest upon the study of man himself; one might suppose that literature, being the expression of man himself, could not do otherwise. History is the record of the doings of man in the world; poetry expresses their soul, political and ethical writings discuss men's principles of life. But the literature of Israel is entirely different; it begins from an entirely different source, not from man, but from God; it keeps God in mind, much more than man, throughout every page. History, to it, is not primarily the record of man's deeds; it is the record of the working of God in the world, and the deeds of men are chiefly of interest as they appear in His sight. Its poetry, from Genesis to the last psalm, is little more than one long chant of the praises of God, and of His dealings with men. Its political principles are governed entirely by the fulfilment of the will of God, its ethics are guided wholly by His commandments. And the consequence of this is remarkable, almost paradoxical. While other literatures remain intensely national, Chinese or Persian, Greek or Roman, the literature of the Old Testament, though even more national than any of these, yet spreads itself out to all conditions and races and times. Their outlook on history, the soul of their poetry, their political and moral teaching, are not confined to themselves alone, much less to any particular generation. They envisage every time and place, because they see all races of men in the same perspective. They reach from God in the beginning to God who is to come again, into the age when, through His coming, the face of the earth is to be renewed. The first sentence of the Old Testament: "In the beginning God created heaven and earth," is the text for all that follows.

In these ways, or rather on account of these contrasts, the literature of the Old Testament differs from and excels all other literatures before the Christian Era; and because of these it has endured while the others have not. Other literatures are very great; they are the expression of the greatest minds the world has known, they have influenced whole races for centuries, and the echo of them has endured in some way down to our own time. They have made use of human language in a way that seems unsurpassed in beauty, in sublimity, and in the expression of truth. But there they stop; they make no claim to go further; for the simple reason that, however great and influential, it remains no more than the greatness and influence of individual men. Confucius and Lao-Tsze, Aeschylus and Plato, Cicero and Virgil, these with a very limited number of names added to them, make up the ancient literatures of China, India, Persia, Greece, and Rome. When we compare them with the peoples they represent, they appear like oases in a vast trackless desert; they speak for a special generation; of the generations before and after them we hear almost nothing at all. Moreover, the literature they produce, the lessons they teach, are essentially individual; though they represent the people from whom they come, still it is their individual greatness that makes a Confucius, or a Buddha, or a Plato, tower above his contemporaries. We know the ancient races more by the things they have done than by the books they have written, by the material stamp they have left on the face of the earth than by the permanent influence they have had on the spirit and soul of the human race. The nation has left its mark, but its voice has been silent; were it not for an individual here and there we might know as little of the soul of ancient China, Greece, and Rome as we know of Babylon or the Egypt of the Pharaohs.

It is quite different with the Hebrew people and their literature, as it is given to us in the Old Testament. It is the literature of a whole people, not that of any individual or individuals; it expresses a whole people's soul, not the mind of one or two great men that have risen in it. While other literatures are known by the names of those who have written them, the writers of the Old Testament are either unknown, or, if they are known, their names count almost for nothing. It covers, moreover, centuries of time; it is not, as with others, confined to a single period. It is genuinely alive, the spontaneous utterance of a whole people in its joys and sorrows; it is not the mere reflection of a few great authors, sitting back and commenting on it. It is more comprehensive than them all; the wisdom of Confucius, the mysticism of Buddha, the moral teaching of Zoroaster, the fine frenzy of Aeschylus, the philosophy of Plato, the sagacity of Cicero, the national enthusiasm of Virgil, the character-painting of Tacitus, the human element in Horace, all find their echo in these few books that, together, make up the literature of Ancient Israel. Nor is it inferior in its expression. The crisp proverbial sentences of Lao-Tsze or the eloquent oratory of Demosthenes, the swelling chorus of the Attic stage or the rolling rhythm of Virgil, the vivid narrative of Thucydides or the parables of Aesop, all may be paralleled from the literature of the Old Testament, and will be found to have there their equal. Indeed, in one point at least, the literature of the Old Testament, as literature only, excels them all. It is more spontaneous, less artificial, less studied, less conscious of itself, more true to life. Other literatures, from their very nature, are men's efforts to say the best they have to say, in the best manner; the Old Testament says its best, in its best way, but without any conscious effort. Its soul is too full to be artificial; its words are too much from the soul to have been carefully chosen; its artistic sublimity lies in the fact that there is no art about it.

These are some reasons why we should claim for the Old Testament, considered only as part of the world's literature and nothing else, not only a place, but a unique place, among the great literatures of the past. But the student who has got thus far will inevitably discover something more. He will find that these books, great literature as they are, yet were never written as literature; they were written for quite another purpose. Other literatures concentrate on man, analyze him, describe his good and his evil, his fascination and his terror, draw his ideal and hold it up before him. The books of the Old Testament study and describe man no less, but the study is wholly directed to a yet greater knowledge. They hold up an ideal, as does the finest poet or philosopher; but its ideal is not drawn from the study of men, it is the ideal of God Himself. On this account the student of literature will acknowledge it to be the greatest of spiritual writing; and yet, paradoxical as it may seem, he will hesitate to place it among strictly spiritual books. He will find that it can be more crudely naturalistic than Aristophanes or Horace, yet all the time will be beholding an ideal far above that of Plato or Virgil. It can be grossly material, in its story and language, yet no one can doubt that it speaks of a life on a plane far removed from that of material earth. It is full of the realization of this world; no books that have been written dwell more on the beauty of creation and all that is in it. No one would say that the Old Testament fails to recognize the world about us, or to give full attention to man with all his strength and his weakness. On the contrary, the rewards and punishments, of men and of nations of men, are almost all pronounced with reference to life upon this earth. And yet all the time the attention is fixed elsewhere. It is not man but God that matters: "Thou shalt love the Lord thy God, with thy whole heart and with thy whole soul, with thy whole mind and with thy whole strength," rings through all the books from beginning to end, as the key to the poetry, and philosophy, and history, and peace, of the life of man on earth. The Old Testament is the most natural of ancient books, yet it is also the most supernatural.

It is this supernatural atmosphere, this divine orientation we may call it, absolutely sure and unchanging from beginning to end as if no other concept of life was to be considered, which differentiates the Old Testament, more than anything else, from all other ancient literatures, whether their books be called national or sacred. But this leads to another discovery; these books were given an authority far beyond that of any other books that have ever been written. Other sacred books, even the best, are recognized as man-made; however sublime they may be, however

they may even be worshipped, as among the inhabitants of
Sindh, yet their contents are accepted as the output of man
alone, the expression of man at his best. It is not so with
the Old Testament, as the Hebrews understood it. It was
not the word of man, but of God Himself, and was spoken
with His authority. Such was the belief of those who lived
by it; and it is precisely this, and not any mere preference
or choice of men, that has given it its influence throughout
the ages. Besides the Hebrews of old, others after them
have come to believe that God and not man was their
author. Before the coming of Our Lord other sacred books
were making new civilizations in Asia, solid and spreading
while Europe was still in darkness; but all have shown that
their sphere was confined. Few have reached beyond the
people among whom they were written, none have been
so universal-minded as to win the world. With the Old Testament, especially when interpreted by the New, it has been
otherwise. Though at first it was jealously guarded by a tiny
nation as something peculiarly its own, still, throughout its
pages the assurance is again and again renewed that it is a
book for all the world to know; its mind, its teaching, its
life will one day be welcomed by Jew and Gentile alike.
What we call our Christian civilization has been built
upon the Bible, on the Old Testament and the New, on
the New as the fulfilment of the Old, on the Old as the
record of that which the New completed and made perfect.
Without the Old Testament, and the certainty of faith, of
the hand of God in all things, of the glory of His service,
which it assumes and teaches, Christian civilization could
scarcely have been the thing it is; Our Lord Himself tells
us that He had come, not to destroy, but to perfect that
which had gone before.

So far, we have tried to estimate the value of the books
of the Old Testament under three headings. *First,* as the

literature of a nation, as a people's expression of itself through the course of its development, they are unique among all the literatures of the time before Christ; and this is true whether we consider their spontaneous expression of a whole people's mind, or the long period of time they cover, or the range of their subject-matter. *Second,* in the purpose of their teaching, they excel all other ancient books. They center wholly on God, and everywhere draw men to Him; they define for men the law of nature, more clearly than it is defined in any other books; they reveal to man a supernatural ideal, lifting him above the material world in which he lives; thus they lay the foundation of a new civilization, stable and solid, which has stood the test of two thousand years. *Third,* because of these, they have provided a moral standard, as well as an outlook, which has shown itself to be adapted to the whole world, of whatever degree, or civilization, or color. Tied to no one nation or race, not even tied to humanity itself, they prove themselves to have come from God, they lead back to God, they teach man to live in God; quite apart from the teaching of revelation, the books of the Old Testament stand alone in ancient literature as an expression of the dealing of God with men, and of man's dealing with God. No other literature so much as attempts to compare with the Hebrew literature in this; it is alone the literature of a people in a peculiar way dedicated to God, however we may choose to explain it.

When we have said this, we have already answered, in part, the second question put to us, that is, the *significance* of the Old Testament. For it is hard to believe that this uniqueness, this overshadowing of God, during so long a period, producing such definite and constant results, should have been either a mere matter of natural evolution, or should have come from some characteristic of the people themselves. Of others it may truly be said that the people produced their own literature, of the Hebrews it would be more true to say that their literature produced them. Their history is that of a people that has been tried by every disintegrating force, yet their Book has kept them together, and has grown with their growth. They have rejected and lost it, they have gone astray, everyone has gone his own way; yet it has brought them again together, and with the revival of the Book they, too, have revived. They have lost their bearings, and it has restored to them the guiding light. They have been scattered over the world, compelled to live among other nations, with other beliefs, other moral standards, other customs, and their Book has kept them secure, or has given them back what for a time they had lost. They may have been reduced to the lowest place among the nations, yet their Book has filled them with a certainty of their mission, and of the future, which nothing has been able to destroy.

Were there no other significance than this in the Old Testament, it would be enough to make it the most significant collection of books in the world. But there is much more; and now we must part company with our non-believing student, however sympathetic, because to us these books have a further and greater significance, which does not fall within the scope of mere literature. We Christians call these books the "Testament"; that is, to us they are a "witness." We call them the "Old Testament"; that is, they are a "witness" to what is contained in the "New"; and it is this fulfilment in the New Testament which gives to the Old its greatest significance of all. The Old Testament, in other words, is chiefly significant because it foreshadows and foretells Him who is described in the New, and the everlasting Kingdom He would found. Christ Our Lord came from the people, and lived as one of the people, who had been brought up upon this Book; in His time it was studied, for good or for evil, as it had never been studied before. He accepted that position; He took his stand upon the teaching of the Old Testament; none showed it more reverence, no one was more familiar with it, again and again He came back to it to prove His own claim. He bade His enemies, who knew their Testament well, to "search the Scripture," and they would find that "these gave testimony of Him." He said He had come "not to destroy but to perfect"; to interpret aright the teaching of the Old Testament, to raise it to a higher level, as the propounder of the Old Law had said He would. At the end of His life we read how careful He was "that the Scripture might be fulfilled," even to the last cry that He uttered on His bed of death.

In this is the final and greatest significance of the books of the Old Testament. Besides the singular unity which had made them read almost as one book, the same ideas developing, never contradicting, as the centuries passed on, there had also run another thread, which had bound them all together. They were prophetic books; explicitly or implicitly by direct prophecy or by type, they told beforehand of Him that was to come, by word or example they recorded signs by which He might be known. In this sense, and for this purpose, perhaps more than for any other, the Jewish people of Our Lord's own time pondered them. The very first books had said that there would come a Redeemer, the offspring of a woman who would crush the serpent's head. This Redeemer would be of the line of Abraham, Isaac, and Jacob. The children of Israel had been in bondage, and had been delivered by Moses; in some way, this would be fulfilled in Him that was to be. Moses had given them the Law, by which they were to live, apart from and above all other nations; he had also said that one day there would come another Prophet, greater than himself, who would give them a New Law, more perfect than the one he had given them. He had instituted sacrifice as the center of their ritual; he had made the offering of the paschal lamb the central sacrifice of all. The High-priest of the sacrifice that was to be would, in His new sacrifice, give to all this an entirely new meaning. He would be a Priest "according to the order of Melchisedech," sacrificing "in bread and wine," yet no less would fulfil the sacrifice of "the lamb offered from the beginning of the world." He would be another Moses, another Joshua, leading His people into a new world flowing with milk and honey, and another Elijah would announce His coming. He would be another David, a son of David, who would sit on David's throne, and of His kingdom there would be no end. In the times of their greatest troubles, though they had brought these troubles on themselves, as Moses had foretold to them they would, yet other prophets had arisen who had revived their hope till nothing could destroy it; telling them that He who was to come would be born of a Virgin mother, that He would be born in Bethlehem, that He would come out of Egypt, that He would be called a Nazarene, that He would take upon Himself the sorrows of men, and would heal their diseases, that He would come to them seated on an ass, that He would be meek and humble, and would not crush a broken reed. One had foretold Him as a Man of Sorrows, the most abject and despised of men; only when all was over were they able to reconcile this with the promise of the all-world-conquering King.

All this, and very much more of the kind, rang through the Old Testament, so that when the time did dawn the question was on the lips of everyone: "Is not this the Christ?"—"Art thou the Christ?"—"Art thou he that is to come?"—"If thou be the Christ, tell us."—"If thou art the Son of God, come down from the cross."—"We have found the Messiah; we have found him of whom Moses and the prophets did speak, Jesus, the son of Joseph, of Nazareth." This is the last and by far the greatest significance of the Old Testament; and even to this day its influence prevails. The faithful Jew who has failed to find the Messiah in Him who has come, still reads his Bible, which is what we call the Old Testament, and looks forward to the day when it will yet be fulfilled. Even yet, after two thousand years of wandering and persecution, the Old Testament, and it alone, still keeps the Jewish people one, as it did in the days of the captivity in Babylon.

CHAPTER III

The Bible in Perspective

JAMES BRENNAN

Introduction: Understanding the Bible

The Bible must be the best known and at the same time the least known book in the world. In terms of statistics it is certainly the world's best-seller. Any list of the "ten (or fifty or hundred) best books" is sure to contain it. People condemned (in parlor games!) to live on a desert island with one book would probably choose the Bible (somewhat unfairly, since it might be objected that it is not a single book but a library!). It has been translated into more languages and dialects than any other book. It has provided inspiration and themes for numerous works of literature, painting, sculpture, and music. Its phrases have passed into the common speech, and its personalities are household names. It is, above all, the Sacred Book of both the Jewish and Christian religions.

But how many people really read the Bible? How many read it through? And of those who do, how many understand it? The Catholic laity in particular have lost contact with the Bible itself. The average person, one feels, is largely indebted to the liturgy of the Mass for his knowledge of Scripture—a knowledge that is only indirect, mediate, fragmentary. It is certainly an excellent thing that he does get so much of the Bible through the readings and prayers of the liturgy, but this kind of knowledge is insufficient because it is unrelated to the source, to the book as a whole.

Even the priest, who acquired a Bible at the beginning of his seminary career, and followed the usual courses of Introduction and Exegesis, may have come to regard it merely as an arsenal of texts for apologetic purposes or as a treasury of quotations for his sermons. If so, he does not know his Bible. It is not enough to borrow texts from Scripture: the lecturer or preacher must be able to expound the word of God from what one might call a position of strength—from an intimate and comprehensive knowledge of the Bible from *Genesis* to *Apocalypse*.

It is particularly the Old Testament which is neglected or avoided by Catholics, who seem to think that it is not a really Christian Book at all, like the second century heretic Marcion, who rejected the Old Testament altogether from the Canon of Scripture, and was duly condemned by the Church.

We are all having the Bible fed to us in a chopped-up form, so to speak; in the extracts of the Sunday Gospels and Epistles, the psalms and lessons of the Breviary (if we are priests), and the innumerable texts that are sprinkled throughout our books of devotion and our prayer-books. To overcome the defects of this casual, fragmentary, un-coordinated knowledge of the Bible we need to read it through, and we need to read it with some idea of its underlying theme.

Many people are put off by its length and complexity. They feel as if they are entering a kind of maze where they are bound to lose their way; or they are deterred by its notorious difficulties and leave it to the scholars. To all these it is necessary to point that the Bible can be read with profit for its story alone—a great spiritual adventure-story with a continuously developing plot that unfolds itself through book after book to a grand climax—the greatest story in the world. To read the Bible like this is to undergo a profound spiritual experience; to be let into the secret of God's design for our salvation; to be brought nearer to God. But to grasp the plot, to see it in its proper perspective, to follow the unfolding of its themes, some sort of guide is necessary, some broad outline of its thematic development and of the relation of the parts to the whole.

1. The Unity of the Bible

The Bible is a sequence of books of various literary types, whose composition dates from about 1200 B.C. down to about A.D. 100, containing history, poetry, drama, biography, letters, and other works in a rich diversity comprising seventy-three books in all. But, underlying this diversity there is a fundamental unity of theme. It is not so much that the Bible was written to a plan, humanly speaking, like a symposium, but that its different books reveal a plan—God's plan of salvation for fallen mankind through the history of a particular race. It is this that gives the Bible its unique character and its meaning—the golden thread that runs through the pattern of its various parts.

How ever else we may think of the Bible—as literature, as legislation, as doctrine—we must see it primarily as history. It is history with a meaning, a direction, a goal that is given to it by its divine Author; the history of man's redemption from Paradise Lost to Paradise Regained; the epic of salvation that is also the history of a people. It is a story that moves on two planes: the one human, historical, relating the history of the race that God chose for the working out of His grand design; the other divine, eternal, from which God watches the progress of that story and intervenes to direct it.

The great unifying theme, then, is the working out of God's promise of salvation through a Chosen People, and the story falls into two parts, called the Old and New Testaments, from the word "Covenant" or "Alliance" (which the Vulgate translates as "Testamentum") which characterised the solemn relationship into which God entered with this People in order to accomplish His plan. These two parts represent the preparation under the Old Covenant, and the realization, under the New Covenant, of man's salvation.

Fundamental also to this history is the idea of Election or Choice. This idea is presented in the clear statement of Our Lord, "Salvation is of the Jews" (John 4:22), and in the whole record of Old Testament history which can be seen as a series of choices. Thus, God chose to save Noah and his family in the Deluge; chose Abraham to be the ancestor of the Chosen People; chose Isaac rather than Ishmael, Jacob rather than Esau to continue the line of descent; chose Moses; chose David . . . the theme of election runs right through the story. God is following out a plan for the salvation of man that Saint Paul was afterwards to call a "mystery"—something that remained hidden until the "fullness of time," when it was realised in the Incarnation, and was misunderstood by the very people who had been chosen to implement it.

2. The Promise

The story begins in *Genesis,* the first of the five books of the Pentateuch, with cosmic proportions ("In the beginning God created heaven and earth . . ."), but it rapidly narrows down, within the space of eleven chapters, to the

Semitic family dwelling in Mesopotamia from which God calls the ancestor of the people that will carry forward His plan for the redemption of humanity. All that has gone before (the Creation of the world, and of man, the Fall, its punishment, the dispersal of the human race), tremendous as it seems in our eyes, and fundamental as it is to our religion, is only a preface to the story which begins with the call of Abraham. Those first eleven chapters have set the scene and explained why man has need of salvation. The theme that links them with what follows is that veiled promise of redemption for fallen man which is found in Genesis 3:15 (the Protoevangelium, as it is called), and is now repeated to Abraham, and, in varying forms, to his descendants until it is fulfilled in Christ. To the key-concepts of Election and Covenant we have now added that of the Promises, and with an eye to these leading-motives we can more easily follow the plot as it unfolds.

The historical part proper of the Old Testament (as distinct from the earlier pre-history) which begins with chapter 12 of *Genesis*—the history of the Chosen People which is also the history of man's salvation—may be seen unfolding in three stages, dominated by three great figures; Abraham, Moses, David (the three names round which Saint Matthew built his genealogy of Christ when he began his Gospel). These three stages of sacred history are summed up in the Promise to Abraham, the Covenant with Moses, and the Kingdom under David. To each of these stages we may also, at the risk of over-simplification, attach a significant aspect of revealed doctrine: to Abraham the idea of the one true God; to Moses God's Law; to David and the Prophets salvation through the Messiah.

The history of the Patriarchs—Abraham, Isaac, Jacob— the earliest ancestors of the Chosen People, is narrated in the rest of *Genesis*. From Abraham, whom God called from Ur of the Chaldees to dwell in Canaan and to receive the Promise of salvation for his posterity, God's choice uses Isaac and then Jacob to carry on His design. With Jacob, also called Israel (i.e. "blessed by God"), we come to the twelve tribes who sprang from his sons, and to the events that led to their sojourn in Egypt where they were to grow and mature into the nation of Israel that will eventually enter the Promised Land (symbol of salvation at this stage in their history). This is the end of the first stage of Israel's spiritual pilgrimage.

Into this pattern of history there is woven the great doctrinal theme of monotheism—of God's one-ness ("The God of Abraham, the God of Isaac, the God of Jacob" is one and the same eternal presence in this history)—which is in such marked contrast to the polytheism of the surrounding pagan world as to make of Israel's religion a thing unique in its time.

3. The Covenant

The next four books of the Pentateuch all centre in Moses, the Law-giver, the Prophet, the Deliverer of Israel. *Exodus* (the "Going-out") tells how the Israelites were led out of Egypt by Moses from the tyranny of the Pharaoh; formally became God's People in the solemn Covenant on Mount Sinai; received the Law of Moses; and were further tried by a long period of wandering in the desert country bordering on Canaan before they were allowed to enter that Promised Land under another leader, because the faith of Moses had faltered.

The other books of the Pentateuch complete the story of Moses and the Law. *Numbers* (so-called from the lists of names with which it begins) continues the story of the wanderings in the desert; *Leviticus* gives the ceremonial and other laws which Moses drew up for the people; *Deu-*

teronomy (the Second or Supplementary Book of the Law) completes the legal code and recounts the last acts of Moses. The second stage of this sacred history has been accomplished: God has given His People the Covenant and the Law.

Dominating all other themes of revelation here we find, firstly, the Law, which is meant to preserve the unique character of the race and to ensure its fidelity to its spiritual destiny; and secondly, the sense of God's providence over His people, symbolized by the miracles of the Red Sea crossing, the Cloud, the Pillar of Fire, the Manna in the desert.

Next to the Pentateuch comes a series of historical books —*Joshua, Judges,* 1 and 2 *Samuel* (or 1 and 2 *Kings* in some Catholic Bibles)—which narrate how the Israelites invaded Canaan under *Joshua,* divided it amongst the Twelve Tribes, settled down there under the regime of the Judges (military leaders of the different tribes), and ultimately acquired a king who was chosen and consecrated by Samuel, the last of the Judges. Spiritually, this period is seen as one of constant struggle against the dangers of idolatry and immorality in a pagan environment—dangers that would frustrate the design of God by alienating His People from the Covenant.

4. The Kingdom

The setting up of the kingdom under Saul (about 1020 B.C.) is the prelude to the third main phase of sacred history; the reign of David, who unified the kingdom, made Jerusalem its capital, and established the dynasty from which the Savior was one day to be born.[1]

---

[1] *Ruth* is a short idyll, set in the period of the Judges, which tells how a Gentile woman came to be part of David's ancestry. She is mentioned in the genealogy of Jesus (*Matthew* 1:5).

Again, the key-concepts appear: God rejects Saul and chooses David, with whom He renews the Covenant, to whom He repeats the Promises. The Kingdom is a more concrete realisation of the Covenant, but it, too, is only temporary, for already the Messianic Kingdom is being foreshadowed. The idea of salvation which is to be connected with a future heavenly kingdom through a personal Savior or Messiah may be seen in many of the Psalms of which David was the author.

The later history of the kingdom is related in 1 and 2 *Kings* (or 3 and 4 *Kings* in some Bibles), together with 1 and 2 *Chronicles* (or *Paralipomenon*) which give a parallel account while stressing the underlying spiritual lesson of the story. Solomon succeeded David, built the Temple, and raised the kingdom to the zenith of its power and prestige. The wisdom of Solomon became proverbial (the book of *Proverbs* was afterwards attributed to him for this reason), and the people basked in his reflected glory; but Solomon himself was revealing human weaknesses, and internal stresses were threatening his regime. After his death the kingdom split into two (about 931): the Northern Kingdom, consisting of ten tribes, calling itself Israel, which lasted till 721, when it was conquered by the Assyrians; and the Southern Kingdom, consisting of the remaining two tribes, Judah and Benjamin, which lasted till 587, when it was finally conquered by the Babylonians. Another turning-point has been reached in the fortunes of the Chosen People: the Kingdom has been destroyed, the People themselves carried into captivity. Note the divine pattern of election again: the tribe of Judah is spared until 587, and though led away into captivity like the other tribes, survives as a unit, while the rest of the tribes are submerged or swept away by invasion and deportation; for it was out of Judah that the Messiah was to come (*Genesis*

49:8-12), and God's design must work itself out both in the triumphs and the failures of Israel's history.

The schism, strife and disaster of this period of Old Testament history is the background of the Prophets— God's spokesmen to His people in this critical epoch. *Elijah* and *Elisha* appear in the Northern Kingdom during the ninth century; *Amos* and *Hosea,* in Israel, together with *Isaiah,* in Judah, during the eighth; *Jeremiah* and *Ezekiel* in the seventh and sixth centuries, during the final disaster and exile of Judah.

The role of the Prophets was to remind the people of their true destiny and of their obligations to God. Weakened by political division and religious decay, the very existence of the nation was now threatened, firstly, from within, by the growth of idolatry and immorality; secondly, from without, by successive invaders, the Assyrians first and then the Babylonians. The Prophets view the invasions, as a divine punishment for the people's infidelity to the Covenant, and use them as a motive to urge them to repent and turn to God as their only hope. Once again we see the spiritual theme: the events of the time must be seen from the divine level; God is punishing only in order to save.

5. The Exile

Ultimately, the punishment came, and it was complete; the whole land was conquered when Nebuchadnezzar finally captured Jerusalem after two terrible sieges (597 and 587) and carried away the flower of the nation (now represented by Judah) into exile in Babylon. "Upon the waters of Babylon there we sat and wept, when we remembered Sion . . ."—the poignant words of Psalm 136 are the plaint of Israel in exile.

The Exile was one of the most profound experiences in

the history of the nation. Historically, it was yet another turning-point: the end of the Davidic Kingdom. From the viewpoint of the divine plan it is now being shown that Israel's destiny is not bound up with an earthly kingdom at all. Spiritually, the Exile was to be further purification of the Chosen People out of which a "remnant" (as Isaiah calls it) was to return from Babylon after Cyrus the Persian had conquered that empire and released the Jews (as they may now be called) from their bondage. This remnant of a purified Israel will establish a religious regime, more loyal to God, more aware of His universal character, more conscious of the need for a Savior.[2]

Isaiah is pre-eminently the prophet of the first (Assyrian) crisis, when the Northern Kingdom was over-run and Judah was temporarily spared; *Jeremiah* of the fall of Jerusalem (over which he composed the *Lamentations*); *Ezekiel* and *Daniel* of the Exile. These spokesmen of God, as with one voice, alternately threatened the people with the consequences of their sins, and encouraged them with the hope of the future restoration. It is in the Prophecies that we see more clearly the great spiritual doctrines of the Bible: God (now seen more than ever as a universal deity); Sin (in the form of injustice, immorality, and idolatry); the Moral Law; Repentance; Salvation; the *Messiah* or Savior. The teaching of *Isaiah* on this last point is strikingly presented in the Child that is to be born of a Virgin (in chapter 7); and the Suffering Servant of God (in chapter 53).[3]

---

[2] Two shorter prophetic books underline the idea of the Universal God: *Jonah* and *Nahum*, both set in Nineveh, the capital of Assyria.

[3] Three books belonging to this period may be mentioned in passing as pious narratives on the margin of the history: *Tobit* (set in Nineveh after the Northern collapse in 721) is a story of God's providence; *Judith* (set in the period of Nebuchadnezzar) is a lesson of confidence in God; *Esther* (set amongst a Jewish colony in Persia) is again a lesson in God's care for His faithful people.

6. The Restoration

The return of the Jews from Exile (about 536), and the restoration of the Temple under Zorobabel (about 530), of the city walls under *Nehemiah* (about 445), and of the Law under *Ezra* (about 398) are related in two companion-books: *Ezra-Nehemiah* (or 1 and 2 *Esdras*). The Covenant given was solemnly renewed, the Law was strictly enforced, and the Chosen People, now without a king or a kingdom, emerge as a more truly religious community.

New prophets—Haggai, Zechariah, Joel, Malachi—encourage the people and point the way to the Messianic Age. There is a deepening of the nation's spirituality and increasing longing for the Messiah who will finally deliver it. The Israel of the New Testament is taking shape.

A new class of biblical literature also appears in this post-exilic period; a literature born of tribulation and suffering, reflective in character, groping towards a more spiritual solution of the problems of life and death. This is the Wisdom Literature, or the "Writings," as the Jews call them in contradistinction to the "Law" and the "Prophets." In these books we see reflected the spiritual longings and frustrations of a people who, having pinned their hopes to a material idea of happiness, had been duly disillusioned, and were still left seeking for an answer to their problems.

Proverbs is a collection of practical rules of conduct, attributed by a literary fiction to Solomon; *Qoheleth* is a meditation on the vanity of human things; the *Song of Songs* is an allegory about Israel's union with God; *Job* is a poetic drama on the problems of the just man's sufferings; *Ben Sira* is a guide to religious and moral teaching; *Wisdom of Solomon* gives Israel's most advanced doctrines about God, life after death, immortality and such subjects. It is the nearest approach to the New Testament in its doctrine, as it is probably the latest book of the Old Testament to be written. To this collection of literature also, by traditional arrangement, belong the *Psalms,* which we have mentioned in connection with David, since he was their chief author, though many of them must have been added to his collection at a later period. In this book we have the essence of Israel's spirituality in poetic form, the sublimest expression of man's worship of God, the prayer-book *par excellence* of both Jews and Christians.

These books, belonging to a period when the march of Israel's history seemed to be suspended, represent the further spiritual development of the Jews, the deepening of their religious consciousness, and the completion of the Old Testament revelation to the point where it will merge with the New.

There the history of the Old Testament and of the long pilgrimage of Israel almost stops short, except for a kind of epilogue—the period of the two books of *Maccabees,* which describe a holy war against the Syrian domination which had followed the collapse of Alexander's empire. Spiritually, the episode is also a struggle against the pagan influence of Greek culture (Hellenism), in which a leading part was taken by the sect of the Pharisees. A passionate longing for the Messiah and a growing expectation of His coming was a feature of this age. It was only intensified by the Roman conquest of Palestine in 63 B.C., when Judah came under the rule of Augustus, and the historical conditions for the birth of the Savior were fulfilled.

The "fullness of time" had come; the Jews were waiting for a Savior; the world at large was spiritually bankrupt; God's plan had reached its goal—the end of that long process of election and testing that had begun with the call of an obscure nomad named Abraham about 1900 years before.

7. The New Covenant

And so, by a natural transition, we pass from the preparation to the realization; from the Old Testament to the New. Once again, the story moves on two levels, beginning on the eternal plane, as *Genesis* did, with the words of Saint John's Prologue: "In the beginning was the Word . . . ," and then descending to the human level of history with Saint Matthew's genealogy of Jesus Christ that traces His ancestry back through David to Moses to Abraham. Thus do the Gospels introduce the long-awaited Messiah, Jesus of Nazareth, the Son of God incarnate, born of the royal line of David, who was to fulfil the Promises and establish a New Covenant with mankind. Four Gospels present a composite picture of the life and teaching of Jesus, culminating in His redemptive death by which He ratified the New Covenant. The Kingdom has come; not the earthly kingdom of Jewish expectations, but the spiritual kingdom of the Church which is itself a preparation for the eternal kingdom of Heaven.

The foundation and early history of this kingdom, the Church, is narrated in the fifth historical book of the New Testament—*Acts* (or *Acts of Apostles*). A collection of apostolic letters, or Epistles, outlines the teaching of the Church of Christ, and, last of all, a book of prophetic vision (*Apocalypse*) gives a glimpse of its final consummation, when the Last Judgment has taken place and the New Jerusalem has been established in Heaven.

That is biblical history in its broadest outlines, seen as the manifestation of God's design for man's salvation. Read with this theme in mind, much that is obscure in the Old

Testament becomes clearer, and its essential continuity with the New can be seen. The history of Israel, thus understood, is seen to have a spiritual significance for all mankind. The Bible is not merely the history of the Jews; it is our history, too. Israel's spiritual pilgrimage through history is the story of every soul's quest for final happiness. We have actually received the salvation that was promised under the Old Covenant, but we need to re-live the experience of guilt, of repentance, of expectation, of hope which only the reading of the Bible can give. The Bible is the book of hope: its message is an antidote to the pessimism and the materialism of our time. "For what things soever were written were written for our learning; that through patience and the comfort of the Scriptures we might have hope" (*Romans* 15:4).

CHAPTER IV

The World of the Bible

DONAL O'CONNOR

1. The Second Millennium B.C.

At the present time, the fashion in epitaphs, as in greeting-cards, is the terse, the laconic: "Cast a cold eye on life, on death. Horseman, pass by." But things were not always so. In 1892 B.C. an Egyptian court official considered his reception of Semite traders was worth portraying on the walls of his tomb at Beni-hasan. He informs us, in hieroglyphic writing, that they brought "black paint for the eyes" but the picture itself gives us a glance-back into the life of Semitic nomads, their trades and their dress, strikingly similar to those described in the Bible as belonging to the time of the Patriarchs.

Such worldly tit-bits, together with countless other finds of archaeology over the last fifty years "confirm the historical accuracy or literary antiquity of detail after detail in the Pentateuch" [1] and rudely upset the most learned theories which saw in the history of the Patriarchs so many pious legends with only a doubtful *fundamentum in re*.[2]

---

[1] Albright, W. F., *Archaeology of Palestine* (Pelican, 1949), p. 224.

[2] It is about eighty years since Wellhausen (who died in 1918), perfecting the work of Reuss and of Graf, dated the oldest part of the Pentateuch, called "J") from 850-750 B.C., the second (E) before 721, and the third, in which the law of Moses was contained, about 621—six hundred years after Moses' death; the last source (P) was dated as before 400 B.C. Scholars since Lagrange's time have recognised that the historical tradition

It was a real world and not a mythical one into which Abram (later Abraham) moved when, in the first quarter of the second millennium, God said to him: "Leave thy country and thy father's home and come into the land I will shew thee. Through thee will all the nations of the earth be blessed."

When Abraham left Haran and set out for the promised land of Canaan he had already seen many of the great kingdoms of the day. As a youth he grew up near the Persian Gulf in the town of Ur with its "sophisticated brick houses," to borrow Sir Leonard Wooley's neat phrase. From this city, with its centuries of Sumerian civilization and its cult of the moon-goddess, the whole family moved up to Haran—a journey of six hundred miles along the winding course of the Euphrates, past the then powerful kingdom of Mari.

The commercial and political life of the city of Mari was being busily entered into the books as Abraham passed here. Luckily, however, the account books were slabs of wet clay on which the wedge-shaped (cuneiform) writing was easily impressed. These tablets were then dried and hardened and could long outlast the soft papyrus, which requires a dry climate as well as careful handling to survive. But behind all the bustle of trade there was dire poverty in the things of the spirit. The prevailing fashion of thought all over Mesopotamia was a rather bleak scepticism, receiving its literary expression in the epic of Gilgamesh. After heroic adventures this hero finds the precious plant of immortality at the bottom of the sea only to be robbed of his treasure by the cunning of a serpent. And so, the horizon of his thoughts must for ever be the stillness of the tomb.

---

of the Bible is older than the literary expression in which we find these historical facts narrated.

The glory of Mari passed away with the rise of Hammurabi of Babylon, about the year 1700 B.C. The legal code of this great king shows many points of resemblance to the Mosaic legislation and naturally the question was asked who borrowed from whom. Without going into the matter, I may repeat a very telling little point which, as far as I know, was first noticed by Albrecht Alt in 1934, viz., that all the Hammurabi laws (and much of the Mosaic legislation) are in the casuistic form, e.g., *"if a man captures a fugitive slave and brings him back to his master, the master of the slave will pay him two sickles"* (Par. 17 of the Code of Hammurabi), whereas the Mosaic laws are unique in their use of the apodictic form, *"Thou shalt not . . ."*

At the north-western tip of Hammurabi's vast kingdom lived the Hittites, a hardy mountain people with a civilization all their own. The Hittites knew how to brew beer and had mastered the technique of smelting the iron ores which enriched the Anatolian mountains. In an age when the common metals were copper and bronze, weapons of strong iron were the counterpart of our nuclear bombs and the light horse-drawn chariot of the Hittites was their most deadly weapon especially from the year 1600 onwards. The Hittite archives at Boghazkoi include four tablets on horse training—an important military text-book in those days. At the great but indecisive battle of Kadesh in 1297 between Hittites and Egyptians, the latter must have been very impressed by the Hittite chariotry because the most graceful study of Hittite horsemanship is on walls of the mortuary temple of the Egyptian ruler Rameses II, who, incidentally, is thought to be the Pharaoh of the Exodus. But the Hittites, soon after this battle, cease to be a leading power and the only Hittites mentioned in the Bible are of no significance. Abraham and his little band of nomads, as they made their way along the Fertile Crescent from Ur to Egypt, do not seem to have come into contact with the great Hittite kingdom.

When Abraham entered Egypt in search of food, that great kingdom was already old in wisdom and strong in armies. Her pyramids professed the deep conviction of a happy after-life. Her military outposts stretched as far north as the old Phoenician town of Gubla (Gebal), which the Greek merchants called Byblos. Here the fine cedars of nearby Lebanon were exchanged for Egyptian papyrus and this writing material, when imported into the Greek papyrus world, got the name *biblos*. Hence our word "Bible." [3]

The Nile, in its annual flood, spread its rich silt over surrounding land, and hunger-stricken Semites (e.g. Abraham and later Jacob's family) came down to the fertile delta of the river for grain.

Yet, this ancient kingdom was severely shaken by an invasion of "men out of Eastern parts," called Hyksos, who swarmed out of Canaan and gained control over northern Egypt from 1720 B.C. until their expulsion about 1580 B.C. In all probability, these Hyksos were largely Semitic and the biblical account of Joseph's rise to power in Egypt fits in admirably into this period. When the expulsion of the Hyksos took place in 1580, the Hebrews remained on as slaves and it was not until about 1250 B.C. that the Lord, with a mighty hand "brought them out of the land of Egypt" under the leadership of Moses.

This great deliverance was to be forever deeply impressed on their national consciousness and to find religious expression in the annual feast of the Pasch. This liberation is the basis of all their dealings with God; this love of God for his people is the root of the covenant (or alliance). The Covenant of Sinai is the great fact which gave

---

[3] L. H. Grollenberg, *Atlas of the Bible* (Nelson, 1956), p. 73.

a unique sense of election to the materially insignificant Hebrew people wandering in the desert. The link between Pasch and Covenant was so close that when Jesus Christ was to establish the New Covenant in His blood, he chose to do it on the feast of the Pasch.

2. A kingdom divided . . . swept away

But the young Israelite nation was scarcely fifty years in its new home when it had to face a major threat to its existence. From the Aegean coast came the "peoples of the sea," among whom the Philistines were the most notable. Their attack ranged all along the coast from Carmel in the north to Egypt in the south, where the records of Rameses III give us a grim picture of a fierce naval struggle about 1190 B.C. between the Egyptian fleet and that of the Peleset (Philistines) and the Theker.

It was from these Philistines that Palestine got its name and there can be no doubt but Philistine influence penetrated deep into the lowlands south-west of Jerusalem, to judge from the abundance of Philistine pottery that has been found there in recent years—wine craters with their twin horizontal handles and beer jugs with strainer spouts to hold back the barley husks. On their ware they printed the swan in red and black over a creamy wash. It reminded them, I suppose, that their strength was in their boats, whose prows were decorated with the swan's head. At the height of their power, every drink was implicitly a toast to the fleet, and the Philistines, as Albright says somewhere, were mighty carousers.

But they excelled too in iron work, and the Bible admits, not without humiliation, that the Israelites had to bring their farm instruments down to the Philistine forges to be sharpened (I Samuel 13:20), because there wasn't a metal worker in the whole of Israel.

But a vast improvement took place under David and especially under Solomon (who reigned 961-922). The Philistine power was broken, and for the first time, the chariot became an important part of the Israelite army, and a period of great commercial expansion began for Israel. However, as we know in our own day, huge armaments and large public buildings have to be paid for. And so, the unwelcome tax-collector begins, at this period, to present himself in the harvest fields, and a census-taker is noting all the young men who can work for the king in the enforced labor groups. A new class distinction becomes noticeable with the emergence of two new groups: the wealthy merchants who now make use of the domesticated camels to transport their goods along the fertile crescent, and the nobility who administered the affairs of government.

But all this peace and prosperity vanished at Solomon's death and was replaced by rivalry between Israel (in the north) versus Judah (in the south)—a most unfortunate division which weakened the chances of national survival in the difficult years which were still to come, when the centre of world power shifted from the Euphrates to the banks of the Tigris.

The city of Ashur, on the Tigris, called after the god of the same name, was to be the heart of the mighty Assyrian empire which saw its golden age under Salmanasar III (died 824 B.C.). This empire extended as far as the silver mines of Taurus and the cedars of Karkar on the Orontes river, this latter region being dangerously close to Israel.

The northern kingdom (Israel) must have trembled at these mighty rumblings, and, in fact, we know from Assyrian inscription (though not from the Bible), that Ahab, king of Israel, took part in the great battle of Karkar in 854 B.C. against Assyria. At this battle, Ahab was joined

by eleven other kings who had small but wealthy kingdoms on the northern borders of Israel. Ahab's contribution to the allied armed forces was 2,000 chariots and
10,000 men—certainly a formidable force in those days,
and a sign, if sign were needed, that Israel realized her
very existence was in the balance.

But Israel's troubles were as much internal as external.
Ahab's wife, Jezabel, was a princess of the wealthy type
and brought to her new home in Samaria, the Canaanite
cult of Baal (literally "Lord") which was sometimes associated with Ashtoreth, the goddess of fertility. The First
Book of Kings weighs heavy with the tragedy of these hap-
penings: "This Ahab . . . defied the Lord's will as no
other had done before him . . . he married Jezabel and,
led away by her, enslaved himself to Baal's worship (I
Kings 16:30-31). Small wonder that God-fearing men in
Israel, under Jehu, brought about a *coup d'état* and tried
to save Israel for the worship of Yahweh. Jehu's foreign
policy was aimed at peaceful co-existence with his powerful Assyrian neighbour. The price that Jehu paid for peace
was probably high and the black obelisk of Salmanasar III
in the British Museum shows on four reliefs the procession of Israelites bearing gold, silver and other precious
gifts as "the tribute of Jehu" at the feet of the emperor.

Even a century afterwards, the Assyrian king Sennacherib could boast: "from the upper sea of the sunset to
the lower sea of the sunrise, every head is bowed at my
feet." From the Mediterranean to the Persian Gulf "the
god Ashur has granted me unrivalled kingship."

The god Ashur. The faith of the Hebrew people in the
one true God must have been severely tested in those difficult years when the mighty Ashur lorded over the whole
earth. It was during these times that God sent his greatest
prophets to preserve the true belief and to nurse it back

to strength in the face of the threat of these fierce[4] Assyrian kings. It is only in the context of these astounding military victories that we can understand the gravity of the position described in the Fourth Book of Kings, when the king Ahaz of Judah had an Assyrian altar built in the temple at Jerusalem.[5] This happened shortly before the terrible calamities of 721 B.C., when the whole kingdom of Israel was wiped off the map after its capital Samaria fell to the Assyrians. The majority of its people were led off never to be heard of again.[6]

The little kingdom of Judah, nestling in the hill country around Jerusalem was now the only witness to the true faith in the whole world. But her position was becoming increasingly difficult, situated as she was between the great rivals for world power. Egypt was going down in strength, and was, at this period, trying to ferment anti-Assyrian feeling in Judah and elsewhere.

Our information is relatively abundant about the secret plots and the comings and goings that started off the revolt of king Hezekiah of Judah against Assyria in 703 B.C. The prophet Isaiah constantly warned his compatriots:

Woe to them that go down to Egypt for help
And rely on horses . . .

---

[4] The walls of the royal palaces with their alabaster reliefs, are more informative than any book on life in ancient Assyria. The king's chief sport was hunting of wild asses and lions. There is a close resemblance to the bull-fight in the final scenes of the lion-hunt. The death-thrust is made (usually by the king himself) with a short sword into the underbelly of the lion springing on the king.

[5] II Kings 16:10. "When king Ahaz went to meet Tiglath-pileser at Damascus, he saw there an altar of which he sent a likeness, with a full account of all its workmanship to the high priest Urijah." On his return to Jerusalem, Ahaz changed the position of the altars in the Temple, giving the new altar pride of place. Tiglath-pileser died in 727 B.C.

[6] The Assyrian colonists who moved in to the depopulated region were the forebears of the Samaritans of Our Lord's time; hence the disfavor in which the true Hebrews of Judah held the inhabitants of Samaria.

But they look not unto the Holy One of Israel
Neither seek the Lord.
—Isaiah 31:1.

The position was much the same a century afterwards, when the Assyrian power was replaced by the new Chaldaean empire with its centre at Babylon. In 606 the Babylonians entered Jerusalem. The year 597 saw another entry after an attempted revolt by the Jews. Finally in 587 there took place the mass deportation of practically the whole population and the destruction of the Temple. The utter desolation is described by the prophet Jeremiah, who, like Isaiah before him, saw in all these calamities the result of unfaithfulness to God:

I will cause to cease among them
The voice of mirth and the voice of gladness,
The voice of the bridegroom and the voice of the bride,
The sound of the millstones and the light of the lamp.
—Jeremiah 25:10.

Nor only were walls and battlements torn down, but the fountains of human happiness were dried up by the fear which made hearts beat fast at the approach of the armies of Nebuchadnezzar (605-562). The homely rhythm in the early morning of the small domestic millstones being turned by the women folk of the house; the lighting of the oil lamp at evening time; these symbols of serenity were no longer noticed by the passer-by, because "with desolation was the whole land made desolate."

3. Preparing the Way

(a) Dispersion

This wholesale "dispersion" (called *Diaspora* in Greek), of the Jewish people gave them time to reflect. The teaching of the prophet Jeremiah, and the observance of the Mosaic laws were the basic factors in the return to spirituality which characterised the Jewish religion in the sixth and fifth centuries before Christ. Unlike the ten tribes who were "lost" after the mass deportations of 721 B.C., the Jewish community in Babylon and elsewhere preserved their religious and racial identity.

When the Chaldaean empire fell to the swift advance of the Persian king Cyrus in 539 B.C., the Jewish communities of the *Diaspora* gradually adopted Aramaic. This was the language of diplomacy and of trade throughout Cyrus's great empire and continued to be the spoken language in Palestine up to Our Lord's time.

A new era of relative peace set in with Cyrus, who, by his edict of 538, allowed the Jews to return to their ancient home and even financed the reconstruction of the Temple out of his own treasury. An Aramaic document (dated 419) belonging to the Jewish community on the island of Elephantine in Egypt shows that the Persian government authorized the celebration of the feast of the Pasch in their own Jewish temple on the island.

This dispersion was to be further increased in the following centuries before Christ and extended as far west as Italy. These Jewish settlements were the first points of contact of the early Christian missionaries, like St. Paul, who themselves were of Jewish stock.

(b) Greek Influence

At length, when Persian rule gave way to Greek power and after the death of Alexander the Great (323), Greek influence penetrated deep into the minds and habits of all the East from Egypt to Persia. Even God's own people were not immune from it.[7]

It was at this juncture that the Greek manner of reclining at meals replaced the older sitting-up position. Greek theatres were built all over the East. The wisdom of Plato and Aristotle (the latter was Alexander's tutor); the elegance of the wealthy city-states in clothes and styles of jewelry; the Greek language itself—all these refinements remained long after the military power of Greece had passed.

But more sinister, to the Jewish mind, was the coming of the Greek gods. Antiochus IV, who considered himself a god and in 169 B.C. called himself *"theos epiphanes"* ("god manifest") later called himself Zeus Olympius and committed the sacrilege of placing Zeus in the Temple in Jerusalem. The long-suffering of the Jews could last no longer. The venerable priest Mathathias, in the village of Modein slew the Syrian officer who was supervising the offering of the pagan sacrifice. He and his sons fled to the mountains and one of his sons, Judas Maccabeus, became the leader and the inspiration of the fight for faith and fatherland, a fight which brought religious liberty in the year 163. But domestic strife continued until a new world-power in the person of the Roman Pompey captured Jerusalem in the year 63 B.C. and Palestine became part of the Roman empire.

Even after the Roman conquest, the Greek language continued to be the language of daily use in most of the Roman empire and was the vehicle of the Good News of

[7] In the city of Alexandria, founded by Alexander the Great, the Jewish community commissioned a group of seventy-two scholars to translate the Bible into Greek. The Septuagint, as this translation was called, was widely used by the Jewish synagogues throughout the *Disapora* and in the early Christian Church.

salvation, when the Christian message was being carried across the world.

(c) The Roman Network of Communications

The Romans themselves, by their discovering how to make real concrete in the first century before Christ, by their mastery of bridge-building and road-making, facilitated the comings and goings of the first Christian missionaries. Even so, sailing was still the faster way of travelling, especially during the fine summer months. Things were different during the winter when stormy weather made the sea too dangerous and the account of Paul's journey to Rome in Acts 27 shows how glad everyone was to be able to break their journey for the winter months at Malta: "And after three months, we sailed in a ship from Alexandria that had wintered in the island . . . and, the south wind blowing, we came to Puteoli . . . and so we went to Rome."

But, even in Paul's time, Greece was still the intellectual centre of the world, and the centre of Greece was Athens. We may not think very highly of the kind of "wisdom" which was accepted at this time. It certainly has little resemblance to the achievements of Plato and Aristotle, to judge from the specimen of it passed on to us by Apollonius: "it is a proof of wisdom to speak well of all the gods, especially at Athens, where altars are set up in honor even of unknown gods." However, Paul made the best of a bad situation (Acts 17:23), and "reasoned" with people not only in the synagogue, but also in the *agora* (marketplace).

Corinth at this time blossomed into one of the greatest sea ports of the world and Julius Caesar rebuilt the city and peopled it with Italians and Greeks.

But the great wealth of these times was very unevenly distributed. There was practically no middle class: on the one hand wealthy traders and government officials and on the other, craftsmen (like Our Lord) and the very poor. Slave-labour was an accepted institution.

The bulk of the population throughout the Roman empire had little education and none of the sophistication of their masters.[8] Their life was hedged around with the difficulties of finding their daily bread, which, in Palestine, as in many other places consisted of wheat or barley bread, dried fish, dried fruit, leeks and beans. Wine, of course, was plentiful, and usually taken mixed with hot or cold water.

The homeric theology of immortal gods and goddesses was still very popular among the masses, whose religious practice was a mixture of symbolic rites and sexual excesses. As one might expect, there were certain classes of people who did very well financially by this gross superstition, e.g., the silversmiths at Ephesus made "no small gain" by selling their gold and silver images of Artemis (Diana), which often weighed from three to seven pounds each. In all the corruption of the times, it is not surprising to find such evils as divorce, child-exposure, and the cruelty of the amphitheatre.

This is the dark world in which the light of Christ shone. It was to the lower classes of Palestine that Christ, Himself a poor man, announced the glad tidings of redemption. Only the Power of God could cleanse the human heart of all its iniquity.

At last, the promises made to Abraham and his Seed

---

[8] Stoicism, advocating moderation, and Epicureanism, extolling the pleasure of mind and body were the two leading thought-systems of the day.

were fulfilled. God had chosen the weak things of this world to confound the strong, and a fisherman from the East came and planted the faith in the heart of the world, where it remains unto this day.

CHAPTER V

"Before Abraham Was . . ."[1]

R. A. F. Mackenzie, S.J.

The first eleven chapters of the Book of Genesis are among the most significant and fascinating parts of the Old Testament. From the literary point of view, they are also among the most baffling. The problem of their interpretation has been put squarely before Catholic exegetes by recent directives—one might almost call them challenges—from the Holy See; first, the Encyclical Letter *Divino Afflante Spiritu*, and then, the celebrated letter (January, 1948) from the Biblical Commission to the late Cardinal Suhard.[2] The Holy Father hopes, and expects, that the present generation of biblical scholars will achieve a great advance in the understanding of this important and mysterious section of the Word of God. And he had indicated the line along which it is to be sought, namely, the more profound analysis of its *genus litterarium* (literary form). Only thus shall we be able to fix, with greater clarity and certainty than before, the doctrine which the hagiographers here intend to convey, and to determine at the same time the degree of "historicity" to be ascribed to these narratives. In fact, the latter question may be re-

---

[1] This is the substance of a paper read at the annual meeting of the Catholic Biblical Association, Lisle, Illinois, August 28, 1952. Its original title was "The *Genus Litterarium* of Genesis 1-11."

[2] *AAS*, 40 (1948), 45-8; *CBQ*, 10 (1948) 318-23. (Cf. Study Guide: chapters VI and VII.)

garded as the most pressing problem to be solved. It is worth stressing that the Biblical Commission states with all possible clarity that it *is* an unsolved problem; so far, no completely satisfactory solution has been proposed. The facile claim of "strict historicity" is as unacceptable as the opposite extreme of "mere myths."

This paper, naturally, makes no presumptuous claim to furnish the sought-for solution to all difficulties. All I have tried to do is to clarify the outline of the solution towards which recent Catholic work seems to be tending,[3] and to test at the same time its agreement with the teachings of the Church on inspiration and, particularly, inerrancy. Special stress will be laid on two points which are of particular importance in discussing *genera litteraria:* the first is the source of the materials employed by the hagiographer, the second, the hagiographer's purpose in his writing.

---

[3] The following are the titles of some recent studies by Catholic authors, treating of our problem: P. Heinisch, *Probleme der biblischen Urgeschichte* (Luzern: 1947); J. Chaine, *Le livre de la Genèse* (Paris: 1948); J. Coppens, *La connaissance du bien et du mal et le péché du Paradis* (Louvain: 1948); "Inspiration et inerrance (l'application du principe)" (unsigned article), *VDBS*, IV (1949), 530-58; Eufrasio di Cristo Re, O.C.D., "I generi letterari e l'Enciclica 'Divino Afflante Spiritu,'" *Questioni bibliche alla luce dell' Enciclica "Divino Afflante Spiritu,"* I (Rome: 1949), 1-30; D. G. Castellino, "Generi letterari in Genesi I-XI," *ib.,* 31-61; G. Rinaldi, C.R.S., "Osservazioni letterarie su Gen. 2-3," *ib.,* 169-83; E. P. Arbez, S.S., "Genesis I-XI and Prehistory," *AER*, 123 (1950), 81-92, 202-13, 284-94; J. Fischer, "Deutung und literarische Art von Gen 6, 1-4," *Alttestamentliche Studien Friedrich Nötscher . . . gewidmet* (Bonn: 1950), 74-85; R. de Vaux, O.P., *La Genèse (La sainte Bible . . . de Jérusalem;* Paris: 1951); A. Robert, P.S.S., "Historique (genre)," *VDBS*, IV, 7-23; *id.,* "Littéraires (genres)," *ib.,* V (1952), 405-21; E. Galbiati, A. Piazza, *Pagini difficili dell' Antico Testamento* (Genova: 1951); Ch. Hauret, *Origines (Genèse I-III)* (3rd ed., Paris: 1952). These last two I had not seen at the time of writing this paper. This summary bibliography (it could no doubt be much enlarged) ignores the abundant and meritorious work of Protestant and other scholars; but this is simply because the problem, as posed, concerns the relation of literary forms to the supernatural charism of inspiration, as this is defined by Catholic theology. In other words, it is ultimately a theological question.

First, however, it will be helpful to consider the general context of these chapters. What is their place in, and relationship to, the Pentateuch as a whole? If we are justified in considering the Pentateuch as a unit—and it has been so considered in both Jewish and Christian tradition—we see that the greater part, roughly four fifths of it, is concerned with the life and work of Moses. It describes his upbringing, his vocation, his career, the Covenant established, through him, between God and the people, the historical setting of that Covenant and its terms. The name *Torah* alone shows sufficiently the light in which the later Israelites regarded the five books. "Law" may be too narrow a translation, but still the main interest is in the terms of the covenant, the instruction on the way of life required of them by their God. The history of the Wandering, and the biography of Moses, are narrated for the sake of their connection with the Law.

But the story of the Mosaic covenant, and the life of Moses himself, begin only with the Book of Exodus. To this Genesis 12-50 provides a background and an introduction, narrating the history of the ancestors of the Hebrew nation, beginning with Abraham, the father of their race. And Genesis 1-11 is preliminary again to the history of the Patriarchs. Before the origins of the Chosen People, it describes the origins of the human race. Thus the whole book may be regarded as an introduction, in two stages, to the main theme of the Pentateuch. In a sense, the Book of Genesis bears the same relation to the rest of the Old Testament as the Old Testament itself bears, for us, to the New. And this character of prologue, secondary to the main theme, deserves always to be kept in mind in any estimate of the origin and function of the Book.

Now to come to the point of the origin of the narratives

contained in these chapters, i.e. the source from which Yahwistic, Israelite narrators took them over and developed them. The decisive fact here is that they deal with pre-Abrahamic events, and that means pre-Israelite and non-Israelite history. It is necessary to remind ourselves that the people of Israel were *Benê Yisrā'êl,* descendants of the grandson of Abraham. Both as worshippers of Yahweh, and simply an an ethno-cultural unit, they are comparative late-comers on the scene of history. Abraham's date is approximately the 18th century B.C. Before that there were many ancient peoples, religions and cultures— but no Israel. And the Old Testament writers are quite aware of this. The collective memory of the Hebrew people had always a vivid recollection of Moses and the Exodus—cf. for instance how the Book of Deuteronomy or the second part of Isaiah dwells on this; less vividly, they knew that Moses had revived or re-created a tradition that went back to the Patriarchs. But beyond the Patriarchs there was no history that was specifically their own. Their *Heilsgeschichte,* the story of how Yahweh had created and cared for them, went back no further than this.

There are three brief summaries of this *Heilsgeschichte,* in Deuteronomy and Joshua. The first, Deuteronomy 6:20ff, goes back only to the Exodus: "We were slaves of Pharaoh in Egypt, and Yahweh brought us out . . ." Deuteronomy 26:5 goes back to the Patriarchs: "A nomad Aramean was my father, and he went down to Egypt . . ." or perhaps better, "My ancestors were nomad Arameans, who went down to Egypt . . ." Finally, Joshua 24:2 goes back to the origins: "In days of old your fathers lived beyond the River, and worshipped other gods; but I took your father Abraham from beyond the River and made him range the whole land of Canaan . . ." That was the starting-point, the self-revelation of Yahweh to Abraham, the latter's vocation and the Promise. Further back than that, Israelite history could not go.

What then is the pre-Israelite source or origin of Genesis 1-11? Here there are several alternatives to be considered. For Christians, and for Jews who believe in the super-natural character of the history of their race, there is always the possibility of direct revelation. We might attribute all the contents of these chapters to a series of revelations vouchsafed, say, to Moses: the Creation, the Fall, the genealogies, the Flood, the Tower of Babel, etc. But this too simple solution obviously does not commend itself—in virtue of the sound theological principle, *miracula non sunt multiplicanda sine necessitate* (miraculous interventions should not be indiscriminately postulated). All the literary characteristics of these narratives suggest a complicated natural origin and development, and it would be mere laziness for the exegete to appeal to miraculous interventions, before he has exhausted all possibilities of scientific explanation. (The scientific explanation, in turn, only the more clearly brings out the irreducible supernatural element, the humanly inexplicable factor which is the concept, or rather intuition, of the nature of Yahweh.) The first historical "revelation" we are sure of is the Call of Abraham; and I would say that no other need be postulated, to explain the religious values of these chapters.

Another possible explanation is that of primitive revelation and tradition; that is to say, that the first human beings received supernatural knowledge of creation, and passed this on to their children along with the story of the Fall; that this information was handed down from generation to generation, with later events added to it as they occurred, to the time of the patriarchs and through their descendants to Moses.

At first glance this is the most natural of all explanations and it is not surprising that by exegetes of earlier generations it was more or less taken for granted. But the objections that can now be raised against it are so grave that it is no longer defended (*salvo errore*) by any professional exegete, and is disappearing even from our manuals. It is not the primitive revelation that makes the difficulty, but its transmission to Abraham's time.

In the first place, there is the period of time that must be allowed between the origin of mankind and the 2d. millennium B.C. A chain of tradition imaginable for the 20-odd generations recorded in Genesis is inconceivable if the interval consisted of thousands of generations and tens or hundreds of thousands of years—as would be the case at least for the story of the Fall. And the science of palaeontology seems to have established that the antiquity of the human race is—not to try to be too specific—of this order of magnitude.

Secondly, there is strong biblical evidence against this view. The tradition of the Israelites expressly recognized that the call of Abraham marked a new beginning in the relationship of mankind to Yahweh. Abraham's relatives, and his ancestors, were not Yahwists and were not monotheists. They worshipped other gods. Now it is quite impossible, or at least it would imply an extraordinary suspension of ordinary laws of psychology and sociology, that the narratives of Genesis 1-11 should have been transmitted for generations, by word of mouth, by people who did not believe in them nor even understand them. One and all, they are profoundly religious stories, expressly shaped to convey the uniqueness of the one God, His ethical demands, and the special situation of mankind before Him. In short, they are characteristically Yahwistic, and would make no sense at all to people who either knew nothing of

Yahweh or regarded Him as just one more god among many. Unless we are to appeal to a series of perpetually renewed divine interventions, we must reject the idea that there was any chain of tradition through which Abraham could have received these Yahwistic narratives.

A third argument can be drawn from the Hebrew coloring, or rather substance, of some of this material. It is not so much that the personages are naturally represented as speaking (and punning in) classical Hebrew, as the fact that the genealogies consist of Hebrew, or at least West-Semitic, names; take away the names and there is nothing left of the genealogy. Yet the Hebrew dialect developed only in the course of the second millennium; and Proto-Semitic, the presumed parent-language, cannot go back more than a few millennia before that.

We come back therefore to the solution that the origin of these narratives, insofar as they can be separated from the Yahwism that now inspires them, must be sought *outside* Israel and *prior* to Israel. And here we must bear in mind still the new beginning which is represented by Abraham. He and his family, migrants from Northern Mesopotamia to the land of Canaan, had as their main cohesive force a brand new and still rudimentary religion. One God had made Himself known to the Patriarch, had promised him protection, blessings and a vast posterity, and required of him and his descendants a unique loyalty. But the group of Abrahamids must have had, as well as this extraordinary belief, a patrimony, so to call it, of traditions, folklore, and myths—the common cultural background of the Semitic milieu from which they came—and in which, for that matter, they continued to move. Now, any firmly held dogma will gradually but surely work on men's minds; and as it tends to be a principle of action, inspiring a certain kind of conduct, so it is a principle of judgment, inspiring certain thoughts. There was no room, in the concepts of a faithful devotee of Yahweh, for other gods than Yahweh as principles of action or grounds of explanation; whatever divine action was to be postulated or observed, in the world or in men's lives, must and could be ascribed only to Him. Thus a process of transformation came to be applied to this common stock of folklore and imagery, till it was completely recast in harmony with the belief in the uniqueness and morality of Abraham's God. In this process, which may have lasted for generations, much no doubt was discarded altogether; and the transformation of the residue was accomplished, in its main lines, long before the oldest parts of the Pentateuch were put in writing.

This is not pure hypothesis. What is *a priori* very probable can be demonstrated *a posteriori* in at least one instance, by the comparison of the Flood story as presented in Mesopotamian sources with the interwoven double account in Genesis. Needless to say, it is not a question of literary dependence of Genesis on the 11th Tablet of the Epic of Gilgamesh; both versions go back to a common stock of Babylonian tradition (to which in this case there is no reason to deny a certain historical foundation), but the Israelite version has been completely re-thought, re-cast, in function of Yahwistic theology and morality. Another example (though this may be a case of later, literary, adaptation) is perhaps the story of the crushing of the heads of Leviathan, attributed in Ugaritic mythology to 'Aliyan Ba'al, but in the Psalms described as part of the creative activity of Yahweh.

I have already ventured to use the word myth, and this calls for some discussion. It is a word *male sonans, piis auribus offensivum* (disturbing to the faithful), when connected with narratives in Holy Writ; and quite rightly so.

The Biblical Commission in 1909 held that it could not be taught that the accounts of Genesis 1-3 were taken from pagan mythologies or cosmogonies. More recently, the Encyclical *Humani Generis,* while conceding that some things in Genesis 1-11 were borrowed from "popular stories," insisted that these borrowings are by no means to be equated (*minime aequanda sunt*) with myths.[4] It seems fair to say that the whole effect of the process I have been describing is to destroy any such "equation," and to stress how profoundly these Hebrew narratives differ from Babylonian or Ugaritic material, which may provide parallels of vocabulary or scenery or even plot.

The simplest definition of myth is "a story about gods." [5] Essentially, mythology is polytheist; two gods are the very minimum *dramatis personae* that will suffice for it. But in the Israelite narratives there is only the one God, Who therefore cannot be acted upon by any other. On the supernatural level, there can be no conflict. Once Yahweh intervenes, the question is settled; what He does is final, irresistible, definitive. Further, there is here no possibility of a story on the divine level only. There are myths from Ras Shamra and Babylon, in which the whole action is performed in the divine world, with gods and goddesses as the

---

[4] *AAS* 42 (1950), 577.

[5] At least, it is thus that the word has traditionally been understood. It is I think regrettable, because confusing, that the phenomenological approach to comparative religion has led to the word's being applied, in cultic-ritual contexts, in terms of function rather than content or origin. From this point of view, a myth is any religious story which is periodically re-presented and (in the intention of the worshippers) *efficaciously re-enacted,* in a ritual form. This is not only a valid concept, it is an extremely rich and illuminating one; but since it includes, as its supreme monotheistic example, the Passion-narrative which is actualized in the Christian Eucharistic liturgy, it is a drastic extension of the old meaning of the word. *Humani Generis,* by the way, in the passage cited just above, uses the word *mythologiae,* not *mythi* (. . . *cum mythologiis aliisve id genus minime aequanda sunt* . . .), and so avoids this possible confusion.

actors; such a *genus* is simply impossible in Israel. All this prehistory deals with human actors, whose proceedings are judged and settled by unconditioned divine action.

Thus if we say that the "origin" of these stories is to be sought outside Israel, that they are "taken from" the mythology of Abraham's ancestors, we must be quite emphatic on the transformation implied in those words. The suppression of gods, and the introduction of the one transcendent Deity, is such a radical modification that the stories become equivalently new creations. What they now have in common with their material source is (to use a dramatic metaphor) the scenery and costumes; the characters, the plot, and the dialogue are different. Thus—in the hypothesis here presented—it is quite inadequate to speak of the "modification," or "purification," of a myth. The myth is not really "taken over" at all—only its imagery and expressions; and these are used to express a truth concerning the one true God.[6]

Indirect evidence of this process may perhaps be found by comparing Ezekiel 28,11-19 with Genesis 2-3. In the former passage the prophet allegorizes the king of Tyre (considered not personally but as the incarnation of his city) as the central figure of a mysterious narrative. As far as it can be made out from this rather corrupt text, there was a being, created glorious and perfect, and specially favored by God in being installed in Eden, the garden of God. The Hebrew text and the Vulgate call this being a guardian *kerūbh;* the LXX distinguishes him from the *kerūbhîm,* without however calling him a man—still less the first man. Anyway, this creature, dazzled by his own beauty, sinned by pride, and for punishment was ignominiously expelled from God's garden.

---

[6] Cf. the excellent statement of this point by L. Ouellette in his article, "Woman's Doom in Genesis 3:16," *CBQ* 12 (1950), p. 395.

There is an obvious resemblance here to the Genesis story, but there are also some very large differences. Some exegetes seem to think that the prophet is freely combining data from Genesis with mythological reminiscences from elsewhere, but this vague explanation is quite insufficient to explain the firmness and self-consistency of the story outline, or the differences mentioned. In Genesis the sinner is a man; in *Ezekiel* a superhuman being. Transgression in one case is disobedience to a specific command; in the other, pride in general. We must say, I think, that the prophet was drawing on a story parallel, so to speak, to the story of the Fall; it was at once simpler, and more highly coloured. Yet it was no myth, for in it Yahweh was the sole Divinity, acting with His usual majesty and justice; it taught a moral lesson very similar to that of Genesis 3. The patristic writers—Origen and St. Augustine, to name the two most illustrious—who understood this as an account of the Fall of Lucifer, surely penetrated its original meaning. Though Ezekiel narrates it, so to speak, *in obliquo,* the substance of the tale is clear enough for us to judge: the same setting and imagery as were drawn upon by the Yahwist for his teaching on the Fall of Man, were adopted by some other Israelite story-teller(s) to clothe the account of the Fall of one of Yahweh's heavenly ministers. Ultimately the two narratives owe their imagery, and the outline of their stories, to a common source; and there seems no reason why this—the material source, we may call it—may not have been a Phoenician myth.

So far, we have concluded that the narrative materials used by the authors of Genesis 1-11 are re-workings of old traditions, already harmonized by Yahwist believers with their theology. The remote material source is the stock of stories and beliefs common to pre-Abrahamic Western Semites. What now was the purpose of the hagiographers in recording these narratives, and how did they further adapt them to this purpose?

First, it must be remembered that the intention of the hagiographers is always, broadly speaking, didactic. They mean to express, and to convey, truths of faith connected with the nature of Yahweh and the character of His action, past or future. Though many single parts of the Old Testament were composed with more limited objectives, the grand purpose of the whole, and of each inspired writer, is the glorification of God and the religious instruction of men. It is the testimony borne by Israel to the things Yahweh has wrought. Therefore, neither history, wisdom, nor song is preserved for its own sake, nor for any purpose of science, culture, or entertainment. The main purpose of Genesis 1-11—which is the same as saying, the main information that it conveys—is to demonstrate that even *before* Yahweh revealed Himself to Abraham, He was exactly what He has remained since: the unique and supreme Lord of the universe. His covenant, His law, His people— all these had historical beginnings, at a point midway in history, so to speak. As remarked above, the Israelites were well aware that other cultures and civilizations were far more ancient than themselves. But if they were late appearing on the scene, Yahweh was not. He was always there. Whatever the traditions and myths of other peoples may have taught, the Israelites knew that their God was and always had been the sole transcendent Reality. Therefore these chapters are, *inter alia,* a deliberate vindication for Yahweh of all the divine activity there ever was: a dispossession, in His favour, of all the "gods of the nations."

Now, the hagiographers' conviction of this truth did not come to them from history. It came to them, ultimately, from the revelation to Abraham—as that rudimentary *datum* was evolved and developed through subsequent theophanies and the teaching of their religious leaders. But it could be illustrated from history—and, in a sense, it had to be, if only to guard against the danger of attributing creation, and the organization of the cosmos, to other gods. What procedure then would the inspired theologians follow? They would collect whatever stories were current about pre-Abrahamic times, and re-tell them so as to demonstrate the real forces at work. This "re-telling," as suggested above, was probably already substantially accomplished in pre-Mosaic times, but the process would be carried further, till the narratives were fixed in their present canonical form.

What conclusions follow from this, with regard to "historicity" in the modern sense? We must say, first, that the hagiographers had no means of checking it, and, secondly, were not even concerned with it. Telling the story of, e.g., the Exodus from Egypt was one thing: there they could appeal to an uninterrupted chain of tradition in their own people. However much its events had been "systematized," and their providential nature concretely expressed, in the telling, still the historical reality of the fact was firmly present in the national memory. But telling the story of the spread of mankind over the inhabited earth was quite another thing. They took their materials as they found them, and were intent solely on the doctrine that they wished to convey—truths about God, about man, and the relations between them. But *truths* is here the operative word. The creative adaptation which produced our canonical chapters was a process of substituting truth for falsehood. Take the simple fact of creation. Neither of the accounts of creation is historical in the modern sense; they do not go back to eye-witness accounts or contemporary documents. But they are very definitely historical in this sense, that they affirm a past event that truly happened.

Being obliged to make it concrete and imaginable, the narrators body it forth, so to speak, one in the plastic and vivid style of other ancient cosmogonies, the other in the more abstract, schematic form of Judaist theology. And both contrive their presentations so as to affirm at the same time other religious truths about the mode of creation.

There is a certain analogy here with the science of prehistory, as it is generally understood. Where the historian deals with the individual case, the single instance, the unique and never-exactly-repeated event, the prehistorian, by the very nature of his material, is limited to "universals" (in other words, is strictly a scientist). He cannot, for lack of documentation, produce a biography, a name, a single situation; he treats of the typical event, the long-term trend, the ecology of a whole population. So our religious prehistorian describes what is typical: this is how Yahweh always acted; this is how mankind habitually behaved. Only, where the modern scientist—unless he is a popularizer—expresses his findings in abstract and generalized terms, the Israelite prehistorian—who is very definitely a popularizer—must make his doctrine comprehensible in the form of individualized narratives. But except for those cases which are necessarily unique—the Creation, the Fall —their historicity is that of "typical occurrence." They happened, not once only, but many times. In this sense, the term of "prehistory" might be applied to this *genus litterarium*. And to that of course must be prefixed the term "religious," to mark its specific difference; it is not Man in his relationship to the material universe that is here studied, but Man in his essential relationship to the Creator and Lord of all, in the ages preceding the historical divine revelation to Israel.

What then are the historical facts, in the modern sense, affirmed by the sacred writers under the guarantee of inspiration? We cannot improve on the formula used by the Biblical Commission in speaking of chapters 1-3: *facta quae christianae religionis fundamenta attingunt.* The fact of creation, the privileged status enjoyed by the first human beings, their fall from grace and their punishment, the continued sinfulness of their race, God's repeated interventions to vindicate justice, along with His never-failing mercy, the continued existence of a virtuous minority—these and the like are the teachings which the hagiographers affirm.

It is not my purpose here to go into more detail; it is sufficient to have sketched, at least, a possible analysis of "religious prehistory," as a *genus litterarium* proper to these chapters of Genesis, which may perhaps help towards solving some of our outstanding problems.

CHAPTER VI

"Divino Afflante Spiritu"

*The Encyclical Letter of His Holiness,
Pope Pius XII, on Biblical Studies and
Opportune Means of Promoting Them, 1943*

TRANSLATED BY
RT. REV. MSGR. CANON G. D. SMITH, D.D., PH.D.

Venerable Brethren and beloved children, Health and
Our Apostolic Benediction.

INTRODUCTION

The Solicitude of the Church for Holy Scripture—
The Golden Jubilee of "Providentissimus Deus"

It was under the inspiration of the Holy Ghost that the
Sacred Writers composed those books which God, in His
fatherly charity towards the human race, has vouchsafed to
bestow in order "to teach, to reprove, to correct, to instruct in justice, that the man of God may be perfect, furnished to every good work." [1] It is no wonder, then, that
Holy Church, having received inviolate from the hands of
the Apostles this heaven-sent treasure, which she esteems
as a most precious source and divine rule of doctrine concerning faith and morals, has accordingly guarded it with

---

[1] *II Tim.*, iii, 16 sq.

every care, protected it from any false and perverse interpretation, and made eager use of it for the work of the supernatural salvation of souls—as is clearly shown by innumerable testimonies in every age.

But in more recent times, in consequence of the special attacks which were being made upon the divine origin of Holy Writ and upon its proper interpretation, the Church has exhibited a correspondingly greater vigour and zeal in its guardianship and defence. Thus the Council of Trent solemnly decreed that these "books in their entirety and with all their parts, as they have been accustomed to be read in the Catholic Church and as they stand in the ancient Latin Vulgate edition, must be accepted as sacred and canonical." [2] And in modern times the Vatican Council in order to condemn false doctrines on inspiration, declared that the reason for which these same books are to be held by the Church "as sacred and canonical is not that, having been composed by human industry they have been subsequently approved by her authority, nor merely that they contain revelation without error, but because, being written under the inspiration of the Holy Ghost, they have God as their author and as such have been delivered to the Church herself." [3]

Later this solemn definition of Catholic doctrine, which claims for these "books in their entirety and with all their parts" a divine authority such as must enjoy immunity from any error whatsoever, was contradicted by certain Catholic writers who dared to restrict the truth of Sacred Scripture to matters of faith and morals alone, and to consider the remainder, touching matters of the physical or historical order, as *obiter dicta* and as having (according to them) no connection whatever with faith. These errors

[2] Sess. IV, decr. 1; *Ench. Bibl.,* n. 45.
[3] Sess. III, cap. 2; *Ench. Bibl.,* n. 62.

found their merited condemnation in the Encyclical *Providentissimus Deus,* published on the 18th November, 1893, by Our Predecessor of immortal memory Leo XIII, who in the same Letter issued very wise ordinances and directions for the safeguarding of biblical studies.

It is fitting that We should commemorate the close of the fiftieth year since the appearance of this Encyclical, which is regarded as the great charter of scriptural studies; and therefore, conformably with the solicitude for sacred sciences which We have professed from the very beginning of Our Pontificate,[4] We deem it opportune to confirm and endorse the wise injunctions of Our Predecessor as well as the prudent measures taken by his successors for the establishment and crowning of his work, and also Ourself to set forth such instructions as the present time seems to demand, so that all the children of the Church who devote themselves to these studies may receive added encouragement in so necessary and laudable a task.

I

RETROSPECT

The Work of Leo XIII: "Providentissimus Deus"

Leo XIII's first and chief care was to expound and vindicate against attack the doctrine of the truth of the Sacred Books. He therefore solemnly declared that no error whatever exists in those cases in which the sacred writer, when treating of special matters, "followed sensible appearances" (as St. Thomas puts it),[5] expressing himself "either metaphorically or in the common manner of speaking current

---

[4] *Sermo ad alumnos Seminariorum . . . in Urbe* (24 June 1939); *A.A.S.* XXXI (1939), pp. 245-251.

[5] Cf. I, q. 70, art. 1, ad 3.

at that time, and current also now in many matters of daily experience, even among the most learned men." For "the sacred writers—or, more properly, the Holy Ghost who spoke through them[6]—did not intend to teach men these matters (namely, the inner constitution of visible things), which are in no way profitable to salvation" [7]; principles, these, which "will usefully be applied also to cognate sciences, and especially to history," that is to say, "by a similar method of refuting the fallacies of opponents and defending the historical credit of Sacred Scripture against their attacks." [8] He further pointed out that error is not to be imputed to the sacred writer "when scribes have made mistakes in copying the text," or "when the true sense of a particular passage remains uncertain"; and, finally, that it is absolutely unlawful "either to restrict inspiration to certain parts of Sacred Scripture alone, or to admit that the sacred writer himself has erred," inasmuch as divine inspiration "of itself not only excludes all error, but as necessarily excludes and repudiates it as God, who is the supreme Truth, is necessarily unable to be the author of any error whatsoever. This is the ancient and unchanging faith of the Church." [9]

This, then, is the doctrine which Our Predecessor Leo XIII expounded with all solemnity, and which We now set forth by Our authority also, enjoining that it be scrupulously maintained by all. Moreover, We charge that the same wise counsels and exhortations which, conformably with the requirements of his time, he associated with that doctrine be observed with equal exactness to-day. At that

---

[6] Augustine, *De Gen. ad litt.*, 2, 9, 20; *P.L.* XXXIV, 270 seq.; C.S.E.L., XXVIII, III, 1, p. 46.

[7] Leonis XIII *Acta*, XIII, p. 355; *Ench. Bibl.*, n. 106.

[8] Cf. Benedict XV, Enc. *Spiritus Paraclitus*, *A.A.S.* XII (1920), p. 396; *Ench. Bibl.*, n. 471.

[9] Leonis XIII *Acta*, XIII, p. 357 sq.; *Ench. Bibl.*, n. 109 sq.

time new and serious difficulties and problems were arising from the prejudices of a widely spreading rationalism,
and especially from the investigation of very ancient records excavated in various parts of the East; and therefore
Our same Predecessor, prompted by the zeal of his apostolic office and anxious to ensure that this noble source of
Catholic revelation should become more securely and
profitably accessible for the benefit of the Lord's flock,
while being at the same time kept safe from any corruption, expressed his earnest desire that "greater numbers
should duly adopt and perseveringly maintain the cause
of the Sacred Scriptures, and that those especially who
have been called by divine grace to sacred orders should
devote more and more diligence and industry to their duty
of reading them, meditating upon them, and explaining
them." [10]

The Biblical School at Jerusalem—
The Biblical Commission

With this end in view the same Pontiff had already com-
mended and approved the Biblical School established
through the zeal of the Master General of the Order of
Preachers at the Monastery of St. Stephen in Jerusalem,
an institution of which he said that "it had already rendered great services to biblical science and gave promise
of even greater" [11]; and in the last year of his life he provided an instrument whereby the studies which he had so
warmly recommended in his Encyclical *Providentissimus
Deus* might be more and more fully developed and promoted with every possible safeguard. For by his Apostolic
Letter *Vigilantiae,* dated 30 October 1902, he instituted a

---

[10] Cf. Leonis XIII *Acta,* XIII, p. 328; *Ench. Bibl.,* n. 67 sq.
[11] Litt. Apost. *Hierosolymae in coenobio* (17 Sept. 1892); Leonis XIII
Acta, XII, pp. 239-241, *vid.* p. 240.

Council or, as it is commonly called, a *Commission,* of eminent men "who would have the special task of ensuring by every means that Holy Writ should everywhere among ours receive that more elaborate treatment which the times demand, and be kept safe, not only from every breath of error, but also from any rash opinions." [12] We, too, following the example of Our Predecessors, confirmed and honoured this Commission in practice by making use of its services, as on several previous occasions, to recall interpreters of the Sacred Books to the sound rules of Catholic exegesis which the holy Fathers, the Doctors of the Church, and the Popes have delivered to us.[13]

Work of the Successors of Leo XIII: Biblical Degrees

It will not be out of place here to record with gratitude the chief and most useful contributions which Our more immediate Predecessors have made to the same end, contributions in which we may see the fulfilment of fruits of Leo's happy initiative. In the first place Pius X, wishing "to establish a sure means of providing an adequate supply of professors qualified by solid and sound learning to teach Holy Scripture in Catholic schools," instituted "the academic degrees of Licentiate and Doctorate in Sacred Scripture, to be conferred by the Biblical Commission."[14] He subsequently issued instructions "concerning the programme of scriptural studies in seminaries," so designed that ecclesiastical students "might not only themselves acquire a profound knowledge of biblical science and a real

---

[12] Cf. Leonis XIII *Acta,* XXII, p. 232 sq.; *Ench. Bibl.,* n. 130-141; *vid.* nn. 130, 132.

[13] *Pont. Comm. de re biblica Litterae ad Exc.mos PP.DD. Archiep. et Ep. Italiae* (20 Aug. 1941); *A.A.S.* XXXIII (1941), pp. 465-472.

[14] Litt. Apost., *Scripturae Sanctae* (23 Feb. 1904); *Pii X Acta,* I, pp. 176-179; *Ench. Bibl.,* nn. 142-150; *vid.* nn. 143-144.

appreciation of its nature and value, but also gain aptitude and skill for the ministry of the divine word and for the work of defending the divinely inspired books against attack." [15]

The Pontifical Bible Institute

Finally, "in order that there might be in Rome a centre of higher scriptural studies to promote biblical learning and subsidiary sciences as effectively as possible and in accordance with the spirit of the Catholic Church," he founded the Pontifical Biblical Institute, which he desired "should provide courses of higher study and be equipped with all the apparatus of biblical erudition"; he also determined its laws and constitution, declaring that he was thereby implementing "the salutary and fruitful purpose" of Leo XIII.[16]

Further Ordinances of Pius XI

All this work was crowned by Our immediate Predecessor of happy memory Pius XI, who, among other measures, prescribed also that none should be appointed "professor of Sacred Scripture in a seminary without having first completed a special course of studies in that subject and duly obtained the academic degrees at the Biblical Commission or at the Biblical Institute." Furthermore, he ordained that these degrees should confer the same rights and produce the same effects as the official degrees in Sacred Theology or Canon Law; and he also enjoined that no one should be granted "any benefice involving the *canonical* obligation of explaining Sacred Scripture to the people unless, in addition to other qualifications, he had

---

[15] Cf. Litt. Apost. *Quoniam in re biblica* (27 March 1906); Pii X *Acta*, III, pp. 72-76, *Ench. Bibl.*, nn. 155-173; *vid.* n. 155.

[16] Litt. Apost. *Vinea electa* (7 May 1909); *A.A.S.*, 1 (1909), pp. 447-449; *Ench. Bibl.*, nn. 293-306; *vid.* nn. 296, 294.

obtained the licentiate or the doctorate in biblical science."
At the same time, after exhorting the Superiors General
of religious orders and congregations and the Bishops of
the Catholic world to send the most suitable of their students to attend the schools of the Biblical Institute and
gain academic degrees there, he confirmed his precept by
example, generously endowing annual foundations for that
purpose.[17]

The Revision of the Vulgate

Moreover, the Benedictine monks having in the year
1907, with the favour and approval of Pius X of happy
memory, "been entrusted with the task of making investigations and studies preparatory to editing the Latin Version of the Scriptures known as the Vulgate," [18] Pope Pius
XI determined to establish on a firmer and more secure
basis this exceedingly long, expensive, "laborious, and arduous undertaking," the great utility of which, however,
had been demonstrated by the valuable volumes already
published. He accordingly built the new Monastery of St.
Jerome in Rome, to be devoted exclusively to this work,
and richly endowed it with library and all other aids to
research.[19]

The Use of the Scriptures Encouraged

We ought here also to record how these Our same Predecessors have, as occasion offered, highly recommended the
study and preaching of the Sacred Scriptures and the de-

---

[17] Cf. Motu proprio *Bibliorum scientiam* (27 April 1924); *A.A.S.*, XVI
(1924), pp. 180-182; *Ench. Bibl.*, nn. 518-525.

[18] Ep. ad Rev. Dom. Aidan Gasquet, 3 Dec. 1907; Pii X *Acta*, IV, pp.
117-119; *Ench. Bibl.*, n. 285 sq.

[19] Const. Ap. *Inter praecipuas* (15 June 1933); *A.S.S.*, XXVI (1934),
pp. 85-87.

vout habit of reading and meditating upon them. Pius X
gave warm approbation to the Society of St. Jerome, whose
object is to encourage the faithful in the laudable practice
of reading and meditating upon the Holy Gospels and to
facilitate it for them in every possible way; he exhorted
the Society to persevere energetically in this undertaking,
which he described as "one of the most useful and timely
of projects," since it did much "to dispose of the sugges-
tion that the Church has any objection to the reading of
the Sacred Scriptures in the vernacular or places any ob-
stacle in the way of the practice." [20]

Moreover, Benedict XV marked the fifteenth centenary
of the death of St. Jerome, greatest of Doctors in the expounding of Holy Writ, by carefully inculcating the teaching and example of that Doctor as well as the principles
and regulations set forth by Leo XIII and by himself; and,
besides other most opportune and memorable recommen-
dations on this subject, also exhorted "all the children of
the Church, and especially clerics, to venerate the Sacred
Scriptures, to read them devoutly and meditate upon them
with perseverance"; declaring that "in these pages is to be
sought the food which nourishes the spiritual life to perfection," and that "the chief use of the Sacred Scriptures
lies in their being employed for the holy and fruitful ministry of the divine word." He also paid a further tribute to
the work of the aforesaid Society of St. Jerome, through
whose zeal copies of the Gospels and Acts of the Apostles
are most widely circulated, "so that there is now no Christian family without them, and all are acquiring the habit
of reading and meditating upon them." [21]

---

[20] Epist. ad Em.mum Card. Cassetta *Qui piam* (21 Jan. 1907); Pii X
Acta, IV, pp. 23-25.

[21] Encycl. *Spiritus Paraclitus* (15 Sept. 1920); *A.A.S.,* XII (1920) pp.
385-422; *Ench. Bibl.,* nn. 457-508; *vid.* nn. 457, 495, 497, 491.

The Response of Biblical Students

But it is not only to these regulations, instructions, and exhortations of Our Predecessors that we must ascribe the advancement which has been made in the knowledge and use of the Sacred Scriptures among Catholics; it is Our pleasing duty to attribute it also in no small measure to the work and labour of all those who have readily complied with these behests, by meditating on the Sacred Scriptures, by their research, writing, teaching, and preaching, and by translating and circulating the Sacred Books. The higher schools of Theology and Sacred Scripture, and especially Our Pontifical Biblical Institute, have already produced and are daily producing many scriptural scholars animated by an intense enthusiasm for Holy Writ, who are enkindling the same ardent enthusiasm in the youthful clergy and diligently imparting to them the learning they have themselves acquired. Not a few of them have promoted and are still promoting biblical science in many ways by their writings also: publishing critical editions of the sacred texts, explaining and commenting upon them, translating them into the vernacular, making them accessible to the faithful for their devout reading and meditation, and studying and utilizing profane sciences which are useful for the interpretation of the Scriptures.

These and other undertakings, such as biblical associations, congresses, weekly conferences, libraries, sodalities for meditation on the gospels—all of which are becoming more and more widespread and successful—inspire Us with the confident hope that the veneration, use, and knowledge of Holy Writ will in the future make universal and uninterrupted progress for the good of souls; on this condition, however, that, undaunted by the difficulties with which this great task, like every human undertaking, will be always attended, everyone maintains more steadfastly, more zealously, and more confidently than ever the method of biblical studies prescribed by Leo XIII, a method more clearly and completely explained by his Successors, and by Ourself corroborated and endorsed, the one secure method which has stood the test of experience.

II

PRESENT CONDITIONS

The Changed Conditions of Biblical Study

It is obvious that the conditions of biblical science and of subsidiary studies have changed considerably in the course of the past fifty years. To mention only a few examples, at the time when Our Predecessor published his Encyclical *Providentissimus Deus* only one or two places in Palestine had been explored by excavations for the purposes of this study. But now explorations of this kind have become much more frequent and, being conducted by stricter methods and with experienced skill, are providing much more abundant and more reliable information. How deeply the better and fuller understanding of the Sacred Books is indebted to such investigations is well known to experts and to all those who devote themselves to these studies. Their importance is increased by the frequent discovery of written records which contribute greatly to our knowledge of the languages, literature, events, customs, and cults of very ancient times. Equally noteworthy is the discovery and examination, so frequent in our own day, of papyri, which have given us very valuable information concerning the literature and institutions, public and private, especially of the time of Our Saviour. Moreover, ancient manuscripts of the Sacred Books have been discovered and edited with skilful care; wider and deeper study has been devoted to the exegesis of the Fathers of the Church; and innumerable examples are throwing light upon the forms of speech, writing, and narrative in use among the ancients.

A Stimulus to Scriptural Scholars

All these are benefits granted by divine Providence to our age, and they serve as a stimulus and an encouragement to interpreters of Holy Writ to make eager use of the great light thus afforded for a closer examination, a clearer explanation, and a more lucid exposition of Sacred Scripture. The fact that the said interpreters have already responded and are still responding with alacrity to this challenge—a fact which We observe with great consolation—is by no means the last or the least of the fruits of the Encyclical *Providentissimus Deus,* in which Our Predecessor Leo XIII, as though foreseeing this new development of biblical science, both summoned Catholic exegetes to their task and also wisely traced out for them its method and program.

To assure the uninterrupted continuance of this work and its more and more successful advancement is Our object in this Encyclical, in which We intend especially to indicate to all what still remains to be done, and in what spirit the Catholic exegete ought to-day to approach this great and noble task, and also to stimulate and encourag anew the labourers who are working so strenuously in th Lord's vineyard.

The Knowledge of Ancient Languages

The study of ancient languages and recourse to the original texts had already been strongly recommended by the

Fathers of the Church, and especially by St. Augustine,[22] to any Catholic exegete who would approach the understanding and explanation of the Sacred Scriptures. But the condition of letters at that time was such that only a few possessed any knowledge of Hebrew, and even that knowledge was imperfect. In the Middle Ages also, when Scholastic Theology was in its most flourishing state, the knowledge of Greek too had become so rare in the West that even the greatest Doctors of that time relied for their explanation of Holy Writ on the Latin Vulgate alone.

In these days, on the contrary, not only is Greek, revived since the Renaissance, familiar to virtually all students of antiquity and literature, but a knowledge of Hebrew and other oriental languages is also quite common among men of letters. Indeed, so many facilities are now available for the learning of these languages that the biblical exegete who failed to make use of them, and thus denied himself access to the original texts, could certainly not escape the stigma of levity and negligence. For it is the duty of the interpreter with the greatest care and veneration to seize eagerly upon every smallest detail of what has flowed from the pen of the sacred writer under God's inspiration, in order to reach a deeper and fuller understanding of his meaning. Let him therefore use every diligence to acquire a more and more thorough knowledge of biblical and other oriental languages, and assist his work of interpretation with all the aids that any branch of philology may supply. This was the aim that St. Jerome strove earnestly to achieve so far as the state of knowledge in his time allowed, and similarly untiring labour and extraordinarily successful efforts were directed to the same end by a number of the great exegetes of the XVIth and XVIIth cen-

---

[22] Cf. e.g., Jerome, *Praef. in IV Evang. ad Damasum*, *P.L.* XXIX, 526-527; Augustine, *De doctr. christ.*, II, 16, *P.L.* XXXIV, 42-43.

turies, although the knowledge of languages was then much less extensive than it is to-day.

By this means, then, the interpreter must explain the original text, for this, being the actual work of the sacred writer himself, has greater authority and weight than any translation, however excellent, be it ancient or modern. And the accomplishment of this task will be easier and more effective if to a knowledge of languages is added a sound skill in the art of criticism applied to the said text.

Textual Criticism

The importance to be attached to such criticism was wisely emphasized by St. Augustine who, among the matters to be impressed upon the student of the Sacred Books, gave first place to the care to procure a corrected text. "The correction of the codices," wrote this great Doctor of the Church, "must be the first and watchful care of those who desire to know the divine Scriptures: incorrect manuscripts must give place to amended ones." [23] This art, known as textual criticism, and employed with great brilliance and success in the editing of profane writings, is very rightly applied to-day also to the Sacred Books, precisely because of the reverence due to the word of God. For its proper purpose and effect is to restore the sacred text as exactly as possible, to eliminate the corruptions due to copyists' errors, and as far as may be to free it from glosses and lacunae, inversions and repetitions of words, and other similar errors which usually find their way into writings which have been handed down over the course of many centuries.

---

[23] *De doctr. christ.,* II, 12; *P.L.* XXXIV, 46.

Modern Progress in This Art

It is true that a few decades ago this criticism was employed by many in a completely arbitrary manner, and frequently in such a way that one would have said that they were using it as a means of introducing their own preconceived opinions into the text. But to-day, We need hardly say, it has achieved such stability and sureness of principles that it has become an excellent instrument for producing a purer and more accurate edition of the word of God; and any abuse of the art can now easily be detected. It is equally unnecessary here to recall, since it is a fact well known to all students of Sacred Scripture, that from the earliest centuries until our present age the Church has set great store by the study of this art.

Critical Editions to Be Prepared by Catholics

Now, therefore, that textual criticism has attained such a high level of perfection, biblical scholars have the honourable though not always easy duty of using every endeavour to procure that, as soon as it is possible and opportune, editions of the Sacred Books and of the ancient versions shall be prepared by Catholics in conformity with these critical standards; editions, that is, in which a scrupulous observance of all the laws of criticism shall be combined with the deepest reverence for the sacred text. And let it be clearly appreciated by all that this long and laborious task is not only a necessary condition for a proper understanding of the divinely inspired writings, but also a bounden duty imposed upon us by filial gratitude to God, who has most providently sent us these books from the seat of His majesty, as the letters of a Father to His own children.

The Latin Vulgate and the Original Texts

And it is not to be supposed that this critical use of the original texts is in any way contrary to the wise prescriptions of the Council of Trent concerning the Latin Vulgate.[24] For the Fathers of that Council, as history testifies, were not only not hostile to the original texts but, on the contrary, expressly desired the Sovereign Pontiff, "for the sake of Christ's flock committed to His Beatitude's care," to ensure that in addition to the Latin Vulgate "the Holy Church of God should possess as the fruit of her own labour also one Greek text and one Hebrew text, each as correct as possible." [25] If the difficulties of the period and other obstacles prevented that desire from being fully implemented at the time, We feel confident that it will now find that more perfect and complete accomplishment which the collaboration of Catholic scholars can give it.

The "Authenticity" of the Vulgate

As for the decree of the Council of Trent requiring the Vulgate to be the Latin version "which all should use as authentic," this, as everybody knows, concerns only the Latin Church and her public use of the Scripture, and obviously in no way derogates from the authority and value of the original texts. For the subject of discussion at that time was not the original texts, but the Latin versions then circulating, among which the Council rightly decreed preference to be given to that version which "has been approved by long use in the Church for so many centuries." Hence this pre-eminent authority, or "authenticity," of the Vulgate was determined by the Council not primarily on

---

[24] *Decr. de editione et usu Sacrorum Librorum; Conc. Trid.* ed. Soc. Goerres, V, pp. 91 sq.

[25] Ibid., p. 29.

critical grounds but rather by reason of its legitimate use in the churches through the course of so many centuries, a use which proves this version to be entirely immune from any error in matters of faith and morals; so that, by the very witness and approval of the Church, it may safely and without danger of error be cited in discussions, lectures, and sermons. Its authenticity is therefore more properly called *juridical* than *critical*.

Consequently the said authority of the Vulgate in matters of doctrine in no way forbids—indeed to-day it almost requires—this same doctrine to be proved and corroborated also by means of the original texts; nor does it forbid the aid of these texts to be generally invoked for the better manifestation and explanation of the true meaning of Holy Writ. Nor, finally, does this same decree of the Council of Trent prohibit translations into the vernacular, made even from the original texts themselves, to be provided for the use and benefit of the faithful and for the easier understanding of the word of God, as We know to have been done in many places laudably and with the approval of the authority of the Church.

The Investigation of the Literal Sense

Well equipped, then, with a knowledge of ancient languages and with the aids afforded by the critical art, the Catholic exegete must approach the most important of the tasks imposed upon him; that of discovering and expounding the genuine sense of the Sacred Books. In discharging this function interpreters should bear in mind that their chief aim must be to discern and determine what is known as the *literal* sense of the words of the Bible, "from which alone," as Aquinas excellently observes, "an argument can be drawn." [26] This literal meaning of the words they must

---

[26] I, q. 1, art. 10, ad 1.

investigate with every care by means of their knowledge
of languages, using the help also of the context and of comparison with parallel passages—aids which are all commonly employed also in the interpretation of profane writings for the clearer understanding of the author's meaning.
But the interpreters of Holy Writ, mindful that they are
dealing with the divinely inspired word whose guardianship and interpretation have been entrusted by God Himself to the Church, must take into equally careful consideration the explanations and declarations of the teaching
authority of the Church, the interpretation given by the
holy Fathers, and also the "analogy of faith," as Leo XIII
wisely enjoins in his Encyclical *Providentissimus Deus.*[27]

The Primacy of Theological Doctrine

And let them be especially careful not to confine their
exposition—as unfortunately happens in some commentaries—to matters concerning history, archæology, philology, and similar sciences. These should indeed be given
their proper place so far as they may be of assistance to
the work of interpretation; but commentators must have
as their chief object to show what is the theological doctrine touching faith and morals of each book and text, so
that their commentary may not only assist teachers of theology in expounding and corroborating the dogmas of
faith, but also be useful to priests in their work of explaining Christian doctrine to the people, and help all the faithful to lead a holy and Christian life.

By giving an interpretation such as We have described,
that is, a primarily theological one, they will effectively
silence those who assert that in biblical commentaries they
find hardly anything to raise their minds to God, nourish
their souls, and foster their interior life, and therefore

---

[27] Leonis XIII, *Acta,* pp. 345-346; *Ench. Bibl.,* nn. 94-96.

maintain that recourse should be had to a spiritual and so-called mystical interpretation. The falsity of this contention is shown by the experience of many who have attained spiritual perfection and an ardent love of God through repeated and prayerful consideration of the divine word, and the same is clearly proved by the constant teaching of the Church and the admonishments of the greatest Doctors.

The Spiritual Sense

It is true that not every spiritual sense is excluded from Sacred Scripture; what was said and done in the Old Testament was wisely so ordained and disposed by God that the past would spiritually foreshadow what was to happen in the new covenant of grace. It is therefore the duty of the exegete to discover and expound not only the proper or "literal" meaning of the words which the sacred writer intended and expressed, but also their spiritual significance, on condition of its being established that such meaning has been given to them by God. For God alone was able to know this spiritual significance, and He alone could reveal it to us. And in fact this sense is declared and taught to us by the divine Saviour Himself in the Holy Gospels; the Apostles, following the example of the Master, exhibit it both in speech and in writing; and it is shown in the perpetual and traditional teaching of the Church, as well as in the most ancient liturgical usage, according to the well-known adage: the norm of prayer is the norm of belief.

Accommodating the Words of Scripture

This spiritual sense, therefore, intended and ordained by God Himself, must be shown forth and explained by Catholic commentators with the diligence which the dignity of the word of God demands; but they must be scrupulously careful not to propound other metaphorical meanings as though they were the genuine sense of Sacred Scripture. For although, especially in preaching, a somewhat wider use of the Sacred Text in a metaphorical sense may be profitable, if kept within reasonable bounds, for illustrating doctrines of faith and commending moral truths, yet it must never be forgotten that such a use of the words of Sacred Scripture is, as it were, extrinsic and adventitious to Holy Writ.

Moreover, the practice is not without its dangers, especially to-day, since the faithful, and particularly those who are learned in both sacred and profane sciences, want to know what it is that God Himself means to say to us in the Sacred Scriptures, rather than what some eloquent speaker or writer is expounding with a dexterous use of the words of the Bible. "The word of God, . . . living and effectual, and more piercing than any two-edged sword, and reaching unto the division of the soul and the spirit, of the joints also and the marrow . . . a discerner of the thoughts and intents of the heart," [28] certainly needs no human artifice or manipulation in order to move and stir the soul. The Sacred Pages themselves, written under the inspiration of the Holy Ghost, abound in their own intrinsic meaning; enriched by divine virtue, they have their own power; graced with supernatural beauty, they shine with their own bright splendour—if only the interpreter explains them so completely and exactly as to bring to light all the treasures of wisdom and prudence latent within them.

---

[28] *Hebr.* iv, 12.

The Study of Ancient Commentaries

In this task the Catholic exegete will be greatly helped by the careful study of the exegetical works of the holy Fathers, the Doctors of the Church, and distinguished commentators of the past. Although sometimes less well equipped with profane erudition and linguistic knowledge than the interpreters of our own time, yet, by reason of the office in the Church with which God entrusted them, they excel in a delicate perception of heavenly things, and in a wonderful keenness of understanding, which enable them to penetrate far into the depths of the word of God and bring to light all that can contribute to explaining the teaching of Christ and to promoting sanctity of life.

It is to be regretted that these precious treasures of Christian antiquity are but too little known to many of our modern writers, and that the historians of exegesis have not yet taken all the measures necessary to give this important matter the careful attention and the esteem that it deserves. We should rejoice to see great numbers devoting themselves seriously to the study of Catholic scriptural exegetes and their works; in this way, by drawing upon the almost unlimited accumulation of riches which they contain, they would effectively contribute to showing more and more clearly how well the ancients understood and explained the divine doctrine of the Sacred Books, and at the same time encourage modern interpreters to follow their example and to borrow opportune arguments from them. Thus will come about that happy and fruitful combination of the learning and spiritual unction of the ancients with the greater erudition and maturer skill of the moderns, which will bring forth new fruit in the field of Sacred Scripture, a field ever fertile and never cultivated enough.

III

PROSPECTS

Contributions To Be Expected from Our Own Age

But our own times too, we have the right to hope, can make their contribution to the more profound and accurate interpretation of Holy Writ. There are many matters, especially historical, which were insufficiently or hardly at all developed by the commentators of past centuries, because they lacked nearly all the information needful for elucidating them. Some examples of the difficult and almost insoluble problems by which even the Fathers were faced, may be seen in the repeated attempts of many of them to interpret the first chapters of the book of Genesis, and in St. Jerome's frequent endeavours to translate the Psalms in such a way that their literal sense (*i.e.,* the sense expressed by the words themselves) might be made clear. There are also other sacred books or texts in which difficulties have presented themselves only in recent times, now that deeper archæological research has given rise to new questions offering occasion for a closer investigation of the subject. It is therefore a mistake to maintain, as some who fail to appreciate the conditions of biblical study do maintain, that nothing remains for the modern Catholic exegete to add to the achievements of Christian antiquity. On the contrary, these times of ours have raised many problems which call for further study and examination and serve as a powerful stimulus to the energy and zeal of the interpreter of to-day.

New Resources To Meet New Problems—
The Nature of Divine Inspiration

For if our age accumulates new problems and new difficulties it also supplies, by God's bounty, new aids and helps to exegesis. Especially noteworthy among these is the fact that Catholic theologians, following the teaching of the holy Fathers and especially of the Angelic and Common Doctor, have investigated and explained the nature and effects of divine inspiration better and more fully than was the custom in past centuries. Starting from the principle that the sacred writer in composing the sacred book is the *organon*, or instrument of the Holy Spirit, and a living and rational instrument, they rightly observe that under the influence of the divine motion he uses his own faculties and powers in such a way that from the book which is the fruit of his labour all may easily learn "the distinctive genius and the individual characteristics and features of each" author.[29]

The Individuality of the Sacred Writer

Let the interpreter therefore use every care, and take advantage of every indication provided by the most recent research, in an endeavour to discern the distinctive genius of the sacred writer, his condition in life, the age in which he lived, the written or oral sources he may have used, and the literary forms he employed. He will thus be able better to discover who the sacred writer was and what he meant by what he wrote. For it is evident that the chief law of interpretation is that which enables us to discover and determine what the writer meant to say, as St. Athanasius tells us: "Here, as in all other passages of the divine Scripture,

---

[29] Cf. Benedict XV, Enc. *Spiritus Paraclitus*, *A.A.S.* XII (1920), p. 390; *Ench. Bibl.*, n. 461.

we must observe the occasion of the Apostle's utterance, and note accurately and carefully the person and the subject which were the cause of his writing, lest ignorance or error concerning these points lead us to misconceive the meaning of the author." [30]

Literary Forms of the Ancient East

But frequently the literal sense is not so obvious in the words and writings of ancient oriental authors as it is with the writers of to-day. For what they intended to signify by their words is not determined only by the laws of grammar or philology, nor merely by the context; it is absolutely necessary for the interpreter to go back in spirit to those remote centuries of the East, and make proper use of the aids afforded by history, archæology, ethnology, and other sciences, in order to discover what literary forms the writers of that early age intended to use, and did in fact employ. For to express what they had in mind the ancients of the East did not always use the same forms and expressions as we use to-day; they used those which were current among the people of their own time and place; and what these were the exegete cannot determine *a priori,* but only from a careful study of ancient oriental literature.

This study has been pursued during the past few decades with greater care and industry than formerly, and has made us better acquainted with the literary forms used in those ancient times, whether in poetical descriptions, or in the formulation of rules and laws of conduct, or in the narration of historical facts and events. It has now also clearly demonstrated the unique pre-eminence among all the ancient nations of the East which the people of Israel enjoyed in historical writing, both in regard to the antiquity of the events recorded and to the accuracy with

---

[30] *Contra Arianos* I, 54; *P.G.* XXVI, 123.

which they are related—a circumstance, of course, which is explained by the charisma of divine inspiration and by the special purpose, the religious purpose, of biblical history.

Divine Words in Human Language

At the same time, no one who has a just conception of biblical inspiration will be surprised to find that the sacred writers, like the other ancients, employ certain arts of exposition and narrative, certain idioms especially characteristic of the semitic languages (known as "approximations"), and certain hyperbolical and even paradoxical expressions designed for the sake of emphasis. The Sacred Books need not exclude any of the forms of expression which were commonly used in human speech by the ancient peoples, especially of the East, to convey their meaning, so long as they are in no way incompatible with God's sanctity and truth. "In the divine Scripture," observes St. Thomas, with characteristic shrewdness, "divine things are conveyed to us in the manner to which men are accustomed." [31] For just as the substantial Word of God became like to men in all things, "without sin," [32] so the words of God, expressed in human language, became in all things like to human speech, except error. This is that "condescension" of divine Providence which St. John Chrysostom so highly extolled and which he repeatedly asserted to be found in the Sacred Books.[33]

The Importance of This Branch of Study

Consequently, if the Catholic exegete is to meet fully the requirements of modern biblical study he must, in ex-

---

[31] *Comment. ad Hebr.*, cap. i, lect. 4.

[32] *Hebr.* iv, 15.

[33] Cf. e.g. *In Gen.* I, 4 (*P.G.* LIII, 34-35); *In Gen.* II, 21 (*Ib.* 121); *In Gen.* III, 8 (*Ib.* 135); *Hom.* 15 *in Joan.*, ad i, 18 (*P.G.* LIX, 97 seq.).

pounding Sacred Scripture and vindicating its immunity from all error, make prudent use also of this further aid: he must, that is, ask himself how far the form of expression or literary idiom employed by the sacred writer may contribute to the true and genuine interpretation; and he may be sure that this part of his task cannot be neglected without great detriment to Catholic exegesis. For—to mention only this example—in many cases in which the sacred authors are accused of some historical inaccuracy or of the inexact recording of some events, it is found to be a question of nothing more than those customary and characteristic forms of expression or styles of narrative which were current in human intercourse among the ancients, and which were in fact quite legitimately and commonly employed. A just impartiality therefore demands that when these are found in the word of God, which is expressed in human language for men's sake, they should be no more stigmatized as error than when similar expressions are employed in daily usage. Thus a knowledge and careful appreciation of ancient modes of expression and literary forms and styles will provide a solution to many of the objections made against the truth and historical accuracy of Holy Writ; and the same study will contribute with equal profit to a fuller and clearer perception of the mind of the Sacred Author.

The Research of Lay Scholars

To this matter also, then, our biblical scholars must pay due attention, neglecting no new information which archæology, ancient history, or the study of ancient literature may provide, and which may serve to throw further light upon the mentality of ancient writers, their processes of thought, and their historical and literary methods, forms, and devices. And the Catholic laity should here ob-

serve that, by devoting themselves with active zeal to anti-
quarian study and research, and by assisting in the measure of their power towards the elucidation of cognate
questions hitherto not fully solved, they will be not only
making a contribution to the advancement of profane
knowledge, but also rendering a very great service to the
Christian cause. For all human knowledge, even other than
sacred knowledge, has an intrinsic worth and excellence of
its own, because it is a finite sharing of the infinite knowledge of God; and it receives an added and nobler dignity,
a consecration as it were, when it is used to shed a brighter
light upon divine things.

Many Problems Already Solved

The progress in the investigation of oriental antiquities
which We mentioned above, and the more careful study
of the original text, as well as the wider and more exact
knowledge of biblical languages and of oriental languages
generally, have with God's help borne fruit in the final
solution of many of the objections which, in the days of
Our Predecessor of immortal memory Leo XIII, were being raised by non-Catholic or even anti-Catholic critics
against the authenticity, antiquity, integrity, and historical
authority of the Sacred Books. Catholic exegetes, using
aright those very weapons of learning which their opponents were frequently abusing, have propounded interpretations which, while being in accordance with Catholic
teaching and true traditional thought, appear at the same
time to have met the difficulties which have either arisen
from recent research and recent discoveries or had been
left for our solution as a legacy from ancient times.

The Credit of the Bible Vindicated

The result has been that confidence in the authority and
historical truth of the Bible, which, in the face of so many

attacks, had in some minds been partially shaken, has now among Catholics been wholly restored; indeed, even among non-Catholic writers there are some who have been led by a serious and impartial examination to abandon the views of the moderns and to return, in some cases at least, to the older opinions. This change is due in great part to the untiring labour of Catholic scriptural exegetes who, undeterred by difficulties and obstacles of every sort, have devoted all their efforts to making a proper use of the contributions made by the research of modern scholars, whether in archæology, history, or philology, towards the solution of new problems.

Many Problems Still Unsolved

But it should cause no surprise to find that not every difficulty has yet been dealt with and overcome, and that the minds of Catholic exegetes are still exercised with serious problems also to-day. This, however, is not a reason for being discouraged. It should be remembered that with human knowledge it is very much as with nature: the growth of undertakings is gradual, and it is only after much labour that the harvest can be reaped. Thus questions which in times past were undecided and unsolved have in our own day at last, with the progress of research, been successfully answered. We may therefore hope that those which now appear to be most complicated and difficult will also, with persevering efforts, at some time find complete elucidation.

Scholars Must Persevere

And if the desired solution is long delayed, even if success is not granted to us at all but perhaps reserved for posterity, let no one complain, because the warning which the Fathers, and especially St Augustine, gave in their time is applicable also to us: namely, that the Sacred Books inspired by God were by Him purposely interspersed with difficulties, both to stimulate us to study and examine them with closer attention, and also to give us salutary experience of the limitations of our minds and thus exercise us in proper humility.[34] And so we need not wonder should it happen that one or other question never finds a really perfect answer, perhaps because it deals with matters which are obscure and too remote from our times and experience, or perhaps because, like other profound sciences, exegesis too may have secrets beyond the grasp of our minds, which will therefore, despite all our efforts, remain undiscovered.

But this state of things must in no wise daunt the Catholic interpreter; prompted by a practical and ardent love of his science, and sincerely devoted to Holy Mother Church, he must grapple perseveringly with the problems so far unsolved, not only to repel the attacks of opponents, but also in the effort to find an explanation which will be faithfully consonant with the teaching of the Church, particularly with the traditional doctrine of the inerrancy of Scripture, while being at the same time in due conformity with the certain conclusions of profane sciences.

The True Freedom of the Sons of God

And let all other children of the Church bear in mind that the efforts of these valiant labourers in the vineyard of the Lord are to be judged not only with fairness and justice, but also with the greatest charity; they must avoid that somewhat indiscreet zeal which considers everything new to be for that very reason a fit object for attack or suspicion. Let them remember above all that the rules and

---

[34] Cf. Augustine, *Ep.* 149 *ad Paulinum*, n. 34 (*P.L.* XXXIII, 644); *De diversis quaest.*, q. 53, n. 2 (*Ib.* XL, 36); *Enarr. in Ps.* 146, n. 12 (*Ib* XXXVII, 1907).

laws laid down by the Church are concerned with the doctrine of faith and morals; and that among the many matters set forth in the legal, historical, sapiential, and prophetical books of the Bible there are only a few whose sense has been declared by the authority of the Church, and that there are equally few concerning which the opinion of the holy Fathers is unanimous. There consequently remain many matters, and important matters, in the exposition and explanation of which the sagacity and ingenuity of Catholic interpreters can and ought to be freely exercised, so that each in the measure of his powers may contribute to the utility of all, to the constant advancement of sacred learning, and to the defence and honour of the Church.

The Condition of True Progress

This true freedom of the sons of God, loyally maintaining the doctrine of the Church, and at the same time gratefully accepting as a gift of God and exploiting every contribution that profane knowledge may afford, must be vindicated and upheld by the zeal of all, for it is the condition and source of any real success, of any solid progress in Catholic science. As Our Predecessor of happy memory Leo XIII very clearly expresses it: "The harmony of minds must be preserved and principles must be safeguarded, if from the different studies of many we are to expect great progress in this branch of learning." [35]

[35] Litt. Ap. *Vigilantiae;* Leonis XIII *Acta,* XXII 237 *Ench. Bibl.,* n. 136.

IV

THE DEVOUT USE OF HOLY WRIT

A Grave Obligation

Anyone who considers the immense labour which for nearly two thousand years Catholic exegesis has undertaken in order to promote an ever more thorough and complete understanding and an ever deepening love of the word of God delivered to us through Holy Writ, will easily appreciate how serious is the obligation incumbent upon the faithful, and especially upon priests, to make copious and holy use of the treasure thus accumulated by the greatest minds through the course of so many centuries. For God did not grant the Sacred Books to men to satisfy their curiosity, or to provide them with an object of study and research; these divine oracles were bestowed, as the Apostle tells us, in order that they might "instruct to salvation by the faith which is in Christ Jesus," and "that the man of God may be perfect, furnished to every good work." [36]

The Duty of the Clergy

Priests, therefore, to whom is entrusted the task of securing the eternal salvation of the faithful, having first studied the Sacred Pages with earnestness and diligence and assimilated them by prayer and meditation, must zealously display the supernatural riches of the word of God in their sermons, homilies, and exhortations. Let them corroborate Christian teaching by passages from the Sacred Books, illustrate it by outstanding examples from sacred history and especially from the Gospel of Christ our Lord;

---

[36] Cf. *II Tim.*, iii, 15, 17.

and, while they carefully avoid those arbitrary and far-fetched accommodations which are an abuse rather than a use of the word of God, let their exposition be so eloquent and so lucid that the faithful will not only be moved to resolve upon the amendment of their lives, but also conceive in their minds a deep veneration for Sacred Scripture.

Let Bishops take every measure to foster and increase this veneration among the faithful committed to their charge, by promoting all those undertakings through which men of apostolic zeal are laudably striving to arouse and encourage among Catholics the knowledge and love of the Sacred Books. Let them favour and assist those pious associations whose object is to circulate copies of the Bible, and especially of the Gospels, among the faithful and to encourage Christian families in the habit of reading them devoutly every day; let them, so far as the liturgical laws allow, effectively commend in word and in practice the modern vernacular translations of Sacred Scripture made with the approval of ecclesiastical authority; and let them either themselves hold, or cause expert preachers to hold, public dissertations on biblical subjects.

Biblical Periodicals

Furthermore, the periodicals which are published with such brilliance and success in various parts of the world, either for the scientific treatment and exposition of questions, or for adapting the fruits of such research to the sacred ministry or to the profitable use of the faithful, ought to find zealous supporters in all the members of the clergy, who should duly recommend them among the various classes and sections of their flocks. The clergy who use these and other similar means which an apostolic zeal and a sincere love of the word of God may suggest as conducive to the same noble end, can rest assured that they will find them an effective help in the cure of souls.

The Teaching of Sacred Scripture in Seminaries

But it is clear that priests will not be able to accomplish all this as they ought, unless they have themselves acquired a practical and enduring love of Sacred Scripture while they were in the seminary. Let the Bishops, therefore, whose duty it is to watch over their seminaries with fatherly care, take heed that here also no effort is spared that may assist to the attainment of the said purpose. Let the professors of Sacred Scripture complete the whole course of biblical teaching in such a manner as to equip young candidates for the priesthood and the ministry of the divine word with that knowledge of Sacred Scripture, and inspire them with that love of Holy Writ, without which the apostolate cannot be rich in fruit.

With this end in view let their exegesis be concerned principally with the theological aspect of the subject, avoiding superfluous discussions and omitting what serves more to satisfy curiosity than to promote true learning and solid piety; and let them set forth this literal, and especially theological, sense so soundly, explain it so carefully, and urge it with such unction, that their students may in some sort share the experience of the disciples of Jesus Christ on the way to Emmaus, who, having heard the words of the Master, exclaimed: "Was not our heart burning within us while he . . . opened to us the Scriptures?" [37] Thus may the future priests of the Church find in Holy Writ a pure and perennial source of their own spiritual life, and at the same time food and strength for the office of preaching which they are to undertake. If the teachers of this most important subject have achieved this in the seminaries,

---

[37] *Luke,* xxiv, 32.

then they may be happy in the conviction that they have contributed very greatly to the salvation of souls, to the advancement of the Catholic cause, and to the honour and glory of God, and that they have accomplished a work most intimately connected with the apostolic office.

The Relevance of Holy Scripture to These Times

If all this of which We have spoken, Venerable Brethren and beloved children, is necessary in every age, it is certainly much more urgently needful in these unhappy times of ours, when nearly all peoples and nations are submerged in an ocean of calamities, when a monstrous war is piling up ruin upon ruin and slaughter upon slaughter, and when, with the fomenting of bitter international enmities, We sorrowfully observe that many are losing the sense not only of Christian moderation and charity, but even of humanity itself. Who else can heal these mortal wounds of human fellowship save Him whom the Prince of the Apostles thus addressed in the fullness of confidence and love: "Lord, to whom shall we go? Thou hast the words of eternal life." [38] To Him, therefore, our most merciful Redeemer, we must use every effort to bring all men back again. He is the divine consoler of those that mourn; it is from Him that all men—as well those who wield public authority as those whose duty it is to pay homage and obey—must learn true righteousness, perfect justice, and generous charity; He, and He alone, can be the firm foundation and rampart of peace and tranquillity. "For other foundation no man can lay but that which is laid: which is Christ Jesus." [39]

---

[38] *John*, vi, 69.
[39] *I Cor.*, iii, 11.

The Author of Salvation Revealed

But Christ, this Author of salvation, will be better known by men, more ardently loved, more faithfully imitated by them, according as they are moved with an eager desire to know and meditate upon Holy Writ, and especially the New Testament. For, as St. Jerome says, "To be ignorant of the Scriptures is to be ignorant of Christ," [40] and "if there is one thing which can keep a man wise during this life and teach him equanimity amidst the afflictions and perplexities of this world, I think it is above all the knowledge and devout consideration of the Scriptures." [41] It is in the Scriptures that those who are weary and oppressed by adversity and sorrow will find true consolation and divine help to suffer with fortitude; it is here, in the Gospels, that Christ is shown to all as the supreme and perfect model of justice, charity, and mercy; here that a lacerated and dismayed humanity finds access to the sources of that divine grace which peoples and their rulers must not disdain or neglect if they hope ever to establish and maintain the peace and harmony of men; here, finally, that all will learn to know Christ, "who is the head of all principality and power," [42] and "who of God is made unto us wisdom and justice and sanctification and redemption." [43]

Words of Congratulation and Encouragement to Biblical Students

After all that We have explained and enjoined concerning the adjustment of scriptural studies to the needs

---

[40] St. Jerome, *In Isaiam, prol.; P.L.* XXIV, 17.
[41] St. Jerome, *In Ephes., prol.; P.L.,* XXVI, 439.
[42] *Col.,* ii, 10.
[43] *I Cor.,* 1, 30.

of the present day, it remains for Us, Venerable Brethren and beloved children, to congratulate with fatherly good will all those biblical scholars who are devoted children of the Church and loyally observe her teaching and ordinances, on being chosen and called to so noble a task, and also to encourage them to persevere with renewed vigour and with all zeal and diligence in the work they have so successfully undertaken.

We have called it a noble task. For what task can be more sublime than to study, interpret, expound to the faithful, and defend against unbelievers the very word of God given to men under the inspiration of the Holy Ghost? This spiritual food gives sustenance to the mind of the interpreter himself, who "is nourished unto the remembrance of faith, the consolation of hope, and the exhortation of charity." [44] "To live amidst these things, to meditate upon them, to know and seek nothing else— is not this in some sort to dwell in the heavenly kingdom while yet on earth?" [45] And let the minds of the faithful too be sustained by the same food and learn therefrom to know and love God for the profit and joy of their souls.

Let interpreters of the word of God, then, give themselves with their whole mind to this holy work. "Let them pray that they may understand." [46] Let them labour to penetrate ever more deeply into the secrets of the Sacred Pages; let them teach and preach and so unlock the treasures of God's word also to others. Let the biblical exegetes of to-day emulate as far as they can the magnificent achievements of those great interpreters of centuries gone by, so that now also as in times past the Church may possess doctors who are eminent in the explanation of Holy

---

[44] Augustine, *Contra Faustum*, *XIII*, 18; *P.L.* XLII, 294; *C S E L*, XXV, p. 400.

[45] Jerome, *Ep.* 53, 10; *P.L.* XXII, 549; *C S E L*, LIV, p. 463.

[46] Augustine, *De doctr. christ.*, III, 56; *P.L.* XXXIV, 89.

Writ, and the faithful thus be brought through their work and labour to comprehend all the light, the lessons, and the joy of the Sacred Scriptures. And may they, too, in the discharge of their truly arduous and important office, "have for their comfort the sacred books" [47] and be mindful of the reward laid up for them; forasmuch as "they that are learned shall shine as the brightness of the firmament; and they that instruct many to justice, as stars for all eternity." [48]

For all the children of the Church, therefore, and particularly for teachers of Sacred Scripture, for the young clergy, and for the preachers of the Gospel, We make fervent prayer that with persevering meditation on the word of God they may taste how good and sweet is the Spirit of the Lord;[49] and, as an earnest of the gifts which heaven will bestow and in witness of our fatherly good will, We grant most lovingly in the Lord to each and every one of you, Venerable Brethren and beloved children, Our Apostolic Benediction.

Given at St. Peter's, Rome, on the 30th day of September, the feast of St. Jerome, greatest of Doctors in the expounding of Holy Writ, in the year 1943, the fifth of Our Pontificate.

PIUS PP XII

---

[47] *I Mac.*, xii, 9.
[48] *Dan.*, xii, 3.
[49] Cf. *Wisdom*, xii, 1.

CHAPTER VII

A

A Response of the Biblical Commission to Cardinal Suhard, 1948

Your Eminence,

The Holy Father has been pleased to entrust to the examination of the Pontifical Commission for Biblical Studies two questions, which have been recently submitted to His Holiness concerning the sources of the Pentateuch and the historicity of the first eleven chapters of Genesis. These two questions with their considerations and propositions have been the object of the most careful study on the part of the Right Reverend Consultors and the Most Eminent Cardinals, Members of the above-mentioned Commission. As the result of their deliberations, His Holiness has deigned to approve the following reply in the audience granted to the undersigned on the 16th of January, 1948.

The Pontifical Biblical Commission is pleased to pay homage to the sense of filial confidence that has inspired this step, and wishes to correspond by a sincere effort to promote biblical studies, while safeguarding for them the greatest freedom within the limits of the traditional teaching of the Church. This freedom has been explicitly affirmed by the encyclical of the Sovereign Pontiff gloriously reigning, *Divino Afflante Spiritu,* in the following terms: "The Catholic commentator, inspired by an active and ardent love of his subject and sincerely devoted to Holy Mother Church, should in no way be deterred from grappling again and again with these difficult problems, hitherto unsolved, not only that he may refute the objections of the adversaries, but also may attempt to find a satisfactory solution, which will be in full accord with the doctrine of the Church, in particular with the traditional teaching regarding the inerrancy of Sacred Scripture, and which will at the same time satisfy the indubitable conclusions of profane sciences. Let all the other sons of the Church bear in mind that the efforts of these resolute laborers in the vineyard of the Lord should be judged not only with equity and justice, but also with the greatest charity; all, moreover, should abhor that intemperate zeal which imagines that whatever is new should for that reason be opposed or suspected" (A.A.S., 1943), page 319; English Edition (Vatican Press), page 22.

If one would rightly understand and interpret in the light of this recommendation of the Sovereign Pontiff the three official answers previously given by the Biblical Commission regarding the above-named questions, namely, that of 23rd June, 1905, on the narratives in the historical books of Holy Scripture which have only the appearance of being historical (Ench. Bibl. 154),[1] that of 27th June, 1906, on the Mosaic authenticity of the Pentateuch (*Ench. Bibl.* 174-177),[2] and that of 30th June, 1909, on the historical character of the first three chapters of Genesis (*Ench. Bibl.* 332-339),[3] one will readily grant that these answers are in no way opposed to further and truly scientific examination of these problems in accordance with the results

---

[1] Cf. C. Commentary 52j.
[2] Cf. C. Commentary 48a-d.
[3] Cf. C. Commentary 48e-l.

obtained during these last forty years. Consequently, the Biblical Commission believes that there is no need, at least for the moment, to promulgate any new decrees regarding these questions.

I.—In what concerns the composition of the Pentateuch, in the above-named decree of 27th June, 1906, the Biblical Commission already recognized that it may be affirmed that Moses "in order to compose his work, made use of written documents or oral traditions," and also that modifications and additions have been made after the time of Moses (*Ench. Bibl.* 176-177). There is no one to-day who doubts the existence of these sources or refuses to admit a progressive development of the Mosaic laws due to social and religious conditions of later times, a development which is also manifest in the historical narratives. Even, however, within the field of non-Catholic commentators very divergent opinions are professed to-day concerning the nature and number of these documents, their denomination and date. There are, indeed, not a few authors in different countries who, for purely critical and historical reasons and with no apologetic intention, resolutely set aside the theories most in vogue until now, and who look for the elucidation of certain redactional peculiarities of the Pentateuch, not so much in the diversity of the supposed documents as in the special psychology, the peculiar processes of thought and expression, better known to-day, of the early Oriental peoples, or again in the different literary style demanded by the diversity of subject-matter. Therefore, we invite Catholic scholars to study these problems, without prepossession, in the light of sound criticism and of the findings of other sciences connected with the subject-matter. Such study will doubtless establish the great part and deep influence exercised by Moses both as author and as law-giver.

II.—The question of the literary forms of the first eleven chapters of Genesis is far more obscure and complex. These literary forms correspond to none of our classical categories and cannot be judged in the light of Greco-Latin or modern literary styles. One can, therefore, neither deny nor affirm their historicity, taken as a whole, without unduly attributing to them the canons of a literary style within which it is impossible to classify them. If one agrees not to recognize in these chapters history in the classical and modern sense, one must, however, admit that the actual scientific data do not allow of giving all the problems they set a *positive* solution. The first duty here incumbent upon scientific exegesis consists before all in the attentive study of all the literary, scientific, historical, cultural and religious problems connected with these chapters; one should then examine closely the literary processes of the early Oriental peoples, their psychology, their way of expressing themselves and their very notion of historical truth; in a word, one should collate without prejudice all the subject-matter of the palaeontological and historical, epigraphic and literary sciences. Only thus can we hope to look more clearly into the true nature of certain narratives in the first chapters of Genesis. To declare *a priori* that their narratives contain no history in the modern sense of the term would easily convey the idea that they contain no history whatever, whereas they relate in simple and figurative language, adapted to the understanding of a less developed people, the fundamental truths presupposed for the economy of salvation, as well as the popular description of the origin of the human race and of the Chosen People. Meanwhile we must practice that patience which is living prudence and wisdom. This is what the Holy Father likewise inculcates in the Encyclical already quoted: "No one," he says, "will be surprised, if all difficulties are not yet solved and overcome . . . We should not lose courage on this account; nor should we forget that in the human sciences the same happens as in the natural world; that is to say, new beginnings grow little by little and fruits are gathered only after many labors . . . Hence there are grounds for hope that those (difficulties) also will by constant effort be at last made clear, which now seem most complicated and difficult" (*Ibid.*, p. 318; Engl. Ed., p. 21-22).

> Your Most Reverend Eminence's,
>> Most humble servant,
>>> James—M. Vosté, O.P.
>>> Secretary of the Pontifical Biblical Commission.

B

Evolution and Polygenism

From "Humani Generis," the Encyclical Letter of Pope Pius XII, 1950

No wonder if this spirit of innovation has already borne poisonous fruit in almost every sphere of theology. A doubt is raised, whether the human reason, unaided by God's revelation and by his grace, can really prove the existence of a personal God by inference from the facts of creation. We are told that the world had no beginning; that its creation was a necessary event, owing its origin to an act of liberality which the divine Love could not refuse. So, too, God is no longer credited with an infallible fore-knowledge, from all eternity, of our free human acts. All this is contrary to the declarations made by the Council of the Vatican.

Thus, the teaching of the Church leaves the doctrine of evolution an open question, as long as it confines its speculations to the development, from other living matter already in existence, of the human body. (That souls are immediately created by God is a view which the Catholic faith imposes on us.) In the present state of scientific and theological opinion, this question may be legitimately canvassed by research, and by discussion between experts on both sides. At the same time, the reasons for and against either view must be weighed and adjudged with all seriousness, fairness, and restraint; and there must be a readiness on all sides to accept the arbitrament of the Church, as being entrusted by Christ with the right to interpret the Scriptures, and the duty of safeguarding the doctrines of the faith. There are some who take rash advantage of this liberty of debate, by treating the subject as if the whole matter were closed—as if the discoveries hitherto made, and the arguments based on them, were sufficiently certain to prove, beyond doubt, the development of the human body from other living matter already in existence. They forget, too, that there are certain references to the subject in the sources of divine revelation, which call for the greatest caution and prudence in discussing it.

There are other conjectures, about polygenism (as it is called), which leave the faithful no such freedom of choice. Christians cannot lend their support to a theory which involves the existence, after Adam's time, of some earthly race of men, truly so called, who were not descended ultimately from him, or else supposes that Adam was the name given to some group of our primordial ancestors. It does not appear how such views can be reconciled with the doctrine of original sin, as this is guaranteed to us by Scripture and tradition, and proposed to us by the Church.

Original sin is the result of a sin committed, in actual historical fact, by an individual man named Adam, and it is a quality native to all of us, only because it has been handed down by descent from him (*Cf. Romans 5:12-19*).

PART 2

Questions on the Individual Books of the Old Testament

1

GOD'S PEOPLE IN EGYPT

References: *Anderson:* Introduction, pp. 1-10, 16-26; *C. Commentary:* 116a-122m; *Cambridge Ancient History; Encyclopaedia Britannica,* articles: Egypt, Babylonia, Assyria, Palestine; *G. Atlas:* pp. 11-26; *Sword:* chapter III, pp. 45-59; *W. Atlas:* pp. 8-22; *Study Guide:* chapters 3 and 4.

Introduction

1. Why is *Deuteronomy* 26:5–10 called the Hebrew Creed?

2. In the following texts from the Prophets and the Psalms, one event is presented as the central one in Israel's history: *Amos* 2:9–10; 3:1–2; *Hosea* 11:1–3; *Ezekiel* 20:5–6; *Jeremiah* 2:2–7; *Psalms* 77:9–55; 135:10–12. What is it?

3. In the light of these passages, why is a knowledge of the ancient Near East so important for a sound study of the Bible?

The Fertile Crescent

4. What happened in the 19th and 20th A.D. centuries to open up our knowledge of the ancient Near East?

5. What are the three principal geographical sections that make up the Fertile Crescent?

Egypt

6. Describe the Nile Valley and explain how Egypt was divided into an Upper and a Lower Egypt.

Mesopotamia

7. Describe the river system of Mesopotamia.

---

* Consult Appendix X for code words used in reference sections.

Palestine

8. Describe the geography of Palestine.

9. Why is the Jordan valley a phenomenon unique in the geography of our planet?

Civilizations

10. When did Mesopotamian civilization arise, what cultural advances did it make before Abraham's time and how did its religious ideals differ from those of the Hebrews?

11. Give a bird's eye view of Hebrew history by showing the relationship of the Hebrews to their powerful neighbors from 1800 B.C. to 63 B.C. (cf. Appendix V.)

2

INTRODUCTION TO THE STUDY OF HOLY SCRIPTURE

References: Smith, *Teachings of the Catholic Church,* Vol. I: pp. 6-9, 27-34; Pius XII, Encyclical, *Divino Afflante Spiritu; Study Guide:* chapter 6; *Guide to the Bible* (2nd ed.): chapter I; *C. Commentary:* various introductory chapters, pp. 1-60, can be helpful; *Sword:* chapters I and II, IV, pp. 1-44, 60-71; *G. Atlas:* p. 27.

Revelation

1. In a true sense, God is said to reveal Himself naturally. In the light of *Psalm 18,* and *Romans* 1:18–20, discuss revelation in this sense.

2. Theologically, when we use this term revelation, we mean supernatural revelation. What elements in its origin, content and purpose conspire to make revelation supernatural?

3. Why can Sacred Scripture be said to be supernatural revelation? (*Hebrews* 1:1–2; *Matthew* 28:18–20.)

Inspiration

4. How do we know which books are inspired?

5. Describe what is meant by "inspiration."

6. What is God's role in inspiration; the sacred writer's?

7. What is the difference between revelation and inspiration?

Inerrancy

8. In what sense can the Bible be said to be free from error?

Literary Form

9. Define the term, literary form.

10. Enumerate the various literary forms to be found in the Bible.

11. How is literary form related to the intended sense of Sacred Scripture?

12. In summary, what would you say is the working principle to be used constantly when you are trying to understand the meaning of Scripture?

3

MOSES: PROPHET AND WONDER WORKER: EXODUS 1–18

Date of events: 1290 B.C.

Readings: *Exodus* 1–18.

References: *Anderson:* chapters 1 and 2, pp. 11-59; *C. Commentary:* 129a-129k; 162c-171d; *Foreword:* pp. 16-19; *G. Atlas,* pp. 40-55; *Sword:* chapter VII, pp. 109-131; *W. Atlas:* pp. 27-31.

Early Life 1–2

1. How was the early life of Moses before his call a providential preparation for the work he was to do?

Prophetic Call 3–4

2. Explain the successive steps in the call of Moses.

3. What was the importance of a name in ancient times?

4. What do the three translations of the name Yahweh tell us about how the Hebrews understood the nature of God?

5. What are the main points of the message (3:16–22) which Moses is to carry to the people of Israel?

Wonder Worker 5–13

6. Describe the fruitless discussions with Pharaoh and the impact made on him by the plagues.

7. Are these narratives of the plagues an objective, photographic report of what took place?

8. How do these narratives indicate the author's use of different sources?

9. What was the supreme event to which these narratives bear witness?

Miracles 14–18

10. What is characteristic of Hebrew thinking on how God governs the ordinary workings of the world and the fate of men?

11. How does Hebrew thinking with regard to the miraculous differ from our modern concept of the miraculous?

12. If there is a natural explanation to the crossing of the Red Sea, the manna, the quail, the water from the rock, then where is the supernatural or miraculous element?

4

THE COVENANT HISTORY: EXODUS 19–34

Date of events: c. 1290 B.C.

Readings: *Exodus* 19–24; 32–34.

References: Cf. 3 and *Documents:* pp. 27–37.

The Journey

1. Trace the route the Hebrews followed from Egypt to Mount Sinai if the evidence for its identification with the modern Jebel Musa is correct.

The Great Theophany and the Sealing of the Covenant—19

2. What is a theophany? Describe the one at Mount Sinai.

3. Why is the analogy of a covenant an apt one to express this new and fundamental development?

The Decalogue 20:1–21

4. Discuss each of the commandments taking into account both their meaning in the particular context in which they were given, and their universal significance.

5. Were men free to do the things forbidden by the Ten Commandments before they were revealed to Moses by God?

The Book of the Covenant 20:23–23:19

6. Was the entire Mosaic code given to Moses at this time, and if not, how can it be called Mosaic?

7. What is the relationship of the Mosaic code to the law codes of ancient Near Eastern antiquity?

8. Discuss briefly what the Mosaic code has to say about public worship: 20:22–26; 23:10–19; slaves, 21:1–11; injuries to persons, 21:12–32 (especially significant is 21:23–25); injuries to property 21:33–22:17; religion and charity 22:18–23:9.

Ratification of the Covenant 24:1-11

9. Explain the significance of Moses' actions at the sealing of the Covenant.

Ritual Legislation 25-31

10. The remainder of this section is concerned with ritual legislation. For our purposes the details are unimportant. Simply pick out an example or two of what this was about and show why this legislation was an essential element of the Sinaitic covenant.

Symbolism

11. In the New Testament and in the liturgy of the Church, we find many consciously drawn parallels with the book of Exodus. Explain how and why the writers of the New Testament see a symbolic relationship between the two members of the following pairs:

the passover lamb	— death of Christ on the Cross
the crossing of the Red Sea	— Baptism
the manna	— the Eucharist
the covenant of Mt. Sinai	— Sermon on the Mount
the ratification of the covenant in blood	— Last Supper

5

NUMBERS—JOSHUA—JUDGES

Date of events: 1290–1020 B.C.

Readings: Indicated in text.

References: *Anderson:* chapters 3 and 4, pp. 60-121; *C. Commentary:* 196a-196g; 223a-226i; 227e-228f; 238d-238m; *Foreword:* pp. 21-24, 26-37; *G. Atlas:* pp. 56-67; *W. Atlas:* 42-43.

Desert Wanderings (c. 1290–1250 B.C.)

Numbers, chapters 9–17; 20–22.

1. Trace the route followed by the Hebrews from Mount Sinai to the border of Palestine.

2. How did the Hebrews symbolize Yahweh's continuing presence with them during these wanderings? (Chapter 9.)

The Historical Books

3. In the Hebrew Bible, the books of *Joshua* and *Judges, I* and *II Samuel* and *I* and *II Kings* are classified as prophetic rather than historical. Why?

4. These books have also been called Deuteronomic history since they were apparently rewritten under the influence of that book. Explain in the light of *Deuteronomy* 11:13–17 and 28:1–16.

The Conquest of Palestine (c. 1250–1200 B.C.)

Joshua, chapters 1–8; 10; 23–24

5. What is the archaeological evidence for the date of the Exodus from Egypt and the conquest of Palestine?

6. What is the Deuteronomic significance of the death of Moses and the great delay before the entry into Palestine? (Cf. *Numbers* 20:7–12; *Deuteronomy* 1:37.)

7. *Joshua* 11:23 and *Judges* 1:27-28 give two different accounts of the conquest of Palestine. What are they and how does the Deuteronomic theme help to explain this difference? (Cf. also *Joshua* 1:1–9; 15:63; 16:10; 23:12–13.)

8. Chapter 24 contains the supreme moment of the conquest. What is it and why?

9. The Book of Joshua contains some difficult passages such as the collapse of the walls of Jericho and the Hebrew policy of total warfare for the glory of God with its cruel destruction of innocent people and their cities. Can you offer any explanation for these?

TRIBAL CONFEDERATION IN PALESTINE
(c. 1200–1020 B.C.)

Judges, chapters 1–8; 11; 13–16

10. When the Hebrews began to settle in Palestine, the Canaanite milieu was both a help to them in acquiring the skills of civilization and a terrible temptation. Explain.

11. Just what was the function of the "judge" during this early period?

12. The four-fold cycle of events recounted in *Judges* 2:6–3:10 gives the general Deuteronomic theme of the book. Explain.

6

I & II SAMUEL; I & II KINGS

Date of events: 1020–922 B.C.

Readings: *I Samuel* 1-3; 7-12; 15-16
 II Samuel 1-7; 11
 I Kings 1-14
 II Kings 17; 21-22

References: *Anderson:* chapter 5, pp. 122-153; *C. Commentary:* 248a-248l; 251c-253d; 258e-260e; 265e; 280g-j; *Foreword:* pp. 34-41; *G. Atlas:* pp. 64-84; *Sword:* chapter VIII, pp. 132-149, chapter IX, pp. 156-168; *W. Atlas:* pp. 47-51.

Origins of Hebrew Kingship

1. What were the military, political and economic conditions that brought the Hebrews to realize that they needed to

be ruled by a king instead of a judge? (Cf. I Samuel 4–6;
13:19–22.)

2. What was the difference between the Hebrew concept of
kingship and that of the surrounding monarchic govern-
ments?

Samuel

3. Samuel represented in his person the transition between
judgeship and kingship. Like many of the people, he was
reluctant for this change to come about. Why? (Cf. I
Samuel 8; Judges 8:22–23.)

Saul 1020–1000 B.C.

4. What were Saul's military, political and economic accomplishments?

5. Show the religious factors at work both in Saul's selection
and rejection. (Cf. I Samuel 9–10; 15; 28.)

David 1000–961 B.C.

6. Explain how David consolidated the kingdom geographi-
cally, politically and religiously.

7. In the light of the linking of the Davidic kingship with
the promise made to Abraham (*II Samuel* 7:8–17), why
does David's reign end so unhappily? (*Cf. II Samuel*
11:2–27.)

Solomon 961–922 B.C.

8. What were Solomon's political, military and economic
accomplishments?

9. Describe Solomon's temple in some detail and show why
his building of it caused him to be regarded as a great
king despite his many weaknesses. (Cf. I Kings 5:1–8:21.)

Division of Kingdom

10. What were the pressures that caused the division of the
Kingdom? (Cf. I Kings 11:1–13; 12.)

11. What religious lesson does the Deuteronomic historian draw from the lives of these kings and the division of the Kingdom, and what did he hope to accomplish among his contemporaries by such a presentation?

7

KINGS; EZRA-NEHEMIAH; MACCABEES

Date of events: 922-63 B.C.

Readings: *I Chronicles* 22; 28-29   *I Maccabees* 1-11
           I Kings   17-22   *Nehemiah* 1-13
          II Kings   2-9; 13-21 *II Maccabees* 9; 12
          Ezra   1-10

References: *Anderson:* pp. 201-215; chapter 14: pp. 430-463; *C. Commentary:* chapters on History of Israel 59a-70h; historical background in introductions to above books and those sections of the *Commentary* dealing with the listed chapters; *Foreword:* pp. 44-47; 54-58; *Sword:* chapter X, pp. 109-188.

The Chronicler's Point of View

1. Books *I* and *II* of *Chronicles* (Paralipomena) and *Ezra-Nehemiah* are the works of someone we call the Chronicler. He reinterprets Hebrew history from a point of view different from that of the Deuteronomic historian. Show how this point of view is illustrated by his passing over the political and military ability of David in *I Chronicles* 28-29, and by his interpretation of the division of the Kingdoms in *I Chronicles* 22.

The Kingdoms Before the Exile 922-721; 922-587

The Elijah and Elisha Cycles

2. Explain how the incident between Micaiah and Ahab over the Syrian expedition (*I Kings* 22) and that between

Elijah and Ahab over Naboth's vineyard (*I Kings* 21)
are good examples of the important, independent role
played by prophets in these times.

3. How does the dramatic contest on Mt. Carmel between
   Elijah and the prophets of Baal and Ashtoreth typify the
   great cultural and religious dangers through which Israel
   was passing at this period? (Cf. *I Kings* 18:21.)

4. The Elisha cycle (*II Kings* 2-9; 13; 14-21) is filled with
   marvelous events. How are we to understand them?

The Exile 721; 587–537 B.C.

5. Explain the events leading up to the final exile of the
   Northern Kingdom in 721 and that of the Southern Kingdom in 587.

6. How did the Hebrews maintain their national and religious integrity in Babylon?

The Return From Exile 537–333 B.C.

7. Why did Cyrus liberate the Hebrews from Babylon after
   his victory in 538?

8. What role did Ezra and Nehemiah play in the material
   and spiritual restoration of the nation?

9. Explain the important role played by the Temple in post-
   exilic Judaism.

10. Post-exilic religious developments in Israel have some-
    times been criticized as "legalistic." What can be said in
    their defense?

Greek Rule and Independence 333–63 B.C.

11. Describe the end of the Persian Empire, particularly in
    Palestine.

12. How did the rivalry between the Greek Seleucids and
    Ptolemies as well as their Hellenizing policies precipitate
    the revolt of the Maccabees?

13. How were the Maccabees and their successors, the Hasmonean dynasty, successful in maintaining independence when the pressures against them should have been overpowering?

8

GENESIS: 1–2:4a CREATION

Date of book: 10th century with 8th century and 6th century revisions.

Readings: *Genesis* 1–2:4a.

References: *Anderson:* chapter 6, pp. 154-182; *ANET,* pp. 3ff., pp. 60ff.; *C. Commentary:* 136a-150a especially; *Creation:* entire; *Foreword:* pp. 6-16; *G. Atlas:* pp. 28-39 (*Gen.* 12–50); *Sword:* chapters V and VI, pp. 72–108; *W. Atlas:* p. 22; *Guide:* chapters 5 and 7; Appendix I-III.

Background of Genesis

1. Science today (e.g., geology, palaeontology, astronomy), advances theories as to the creation of the world. Do these theories contradict the *Genesis* account of creation?

2. There are other accounts of creation in ancient Near Eastern literature, e.g., the Egyptian creation texts and the *Enuma Elish*. Why, then, in comparing them with Genesis would you say that the *Genesis* account is unique?

3. The whole creation story in *Genesis* presupposes the Hebrew cosmogony or world picture. How would a Hebrew draw a map of the "world" or "universe"?

Literary Form

4. The framework of the *Genesis* creation story is that of six days (the Hexaemeron). Chart this out in two parallel columns, including what was created on each day.

5. What liturgical purpose leads the author to give us this six day division?

6. Is the order in which things were created in this account, with light being made before the sun, for example, a chronological or logical order?

7. In the light of the above, could you explain the literary form of the Creation story? Is it historical in our sense of the word?

The Text

8. *Genesis* 1:1—The word "create" is used here. Did this mean "make out of nothing" to the Hebrews? (Cf. Gen. 1:2.)

9. *Genesis* 1:14–18—Is there any special purpose behind the *Genesis* account of the creation of the sun, the moon and the stars?

10. *Genesis* 1:26—Does the phrase "let *us* make man," give us an Old Testament glimpse into the mystery of the Trinity?

11. *Genesis* 1:26—How is man like God and how does he differ from the rest of creation?

12. *Genesis* 2:2—If God is omnipotent and a pure spirit, why is he presented here as needing rest?

Revealed Doctrine

13. From this ancient oriental account, certain doctrinal *certainties* emerge about the nature of God, of man and of the world. What are they?

9

GENESIS: 2:4b, ff. MAN, EVE, PARADISE

Date of book: 10th century with 8th century and 6th century revisions.

Readings: *Genesis* 2:4b and following, i.e., to 2:25.

References: Cf. 8.

Background

1. What are the parallels between the literary presentation of *Genesis* 2:4b, ff. and Mesopotamian mythology (e.g., *Enuma Elish*)? (Cf. Appendix I.)

2. Explain the differences between the doctrine of *Genesis* 2:4b, ff., *Genesis* 1:26-28 and that of the *Gilgamesh Epic*. (Cf. Appendix I.)

3. Compare *Genesis* 2:4-5 with the opening lines of the *Enuma Elish,* noting the technique of negation. (Cf. *Proverbs* 8:24.)

Literary Form

4. Compare the style and teaching of *Genesis* 2:4b, ff. with chapters 1-2:4a.

5. The second creation story uses the Yahwist tradition as its source. Give some examples from *Genesis* 2 of the general characteristics of this tradition.

The Text

6. Can we locate the Garden of Eden?

7. *Genesis* 2:7—"Breath of life." Did the Hebrew think of this as the soul?

8. *Genesis* 2:7—"Clay of the ground." Did God make man literally out of the clay of the ground?

9. *Genesis* 2:9—What is meant by the "tree of life"?

10. *Genesis* 2:9, 17, and 3:1–7—What is meant by the "tree of knowledge of good and evil"?

11. *Genesis* 2:17—Adam and Eve were gifted with immortality if they did not sin. Explain.

12. Was Eve literally created from Adam's rib?

Revealed Doctrine

13. What does *Genesis* 2:4b, ff. teach about God, man and lower creation?

10

GENESIS: 3: THE FALL OF MAN

Date of book: 10th century with 8th century and 6th century revisions.

Readings: *Genesis* 3.

References: Cf. 8.

Background

1. The literatures of ancient peoples showed a concern with the problems of suffering and death. Why is the sacred writer's solution to these problems so unique?

Literary Form

2. This chapter is symbolic history. How does this differ from strict history, from allegory or a fictitious story?

The Text

3. *Genesis* 3:1—Do we know from *this* text that the Serpent is synonymous with the forces of evil or the devil?

4. *Genesis* 3:2-6—Show how the dialogue between the Serpent and Eve is a masterful and subtle commentary on the psychology of temptation.

5. *Genesis* 3:7-11—What connection does the sacred writer see between the sin of our first parents and their realization and shame that they were naked?

6. *Genesis* 3:14-24—What punishments does God assign to the Serpent, to Eve and to Adam, and how does the punishment in each instance fit the crime?

7. *Genesis* 3:15—What is the literal meaning of this text, and why is it called the Protoevangelium?

8. In the light of chapter 3 and 2:7, discuss the modern Catholic attitude towards (a) evolution (b) the evolution of man (c) the unity of the human race and (d) the problem of prehistoric man.

Revealed Doctrine

9. What light does this story of the fall of our first parents throw on the nature of God?

10. What sin did Adam and Eve commit?

11. Someone has said that in this whole matter it is more profitable for us to think about our own state of redemption from original sin, about which we know a great deal, rather than dwell on the original sin committed by Adam about which we know very little. Do you agree?

12. Is it not too daring for St. Augustine and the liturgy of Holy Saturday to call Adam and Eve's sin "blessed"? (Cf. Offertory Prayer of Mass.)

11

PREHISTORIC CIVILIZATION—THE PATRIARCHS: GENESIS 4–11; 12–50

Date of book: 10th century with 8th century and 6th century revisions.

Readings: *Genesis* 4–11; 12, 15, 19, 24–29; 45–48.

References: Prehistoric Civilization: Cf. 8; *Appendix* II and III. The Patriarchs: *Anderson:* pp. 173-182.

Prehistoric Civilization (Genesis 4–11)

Cain and Abel Genesis 4

1. Doesn't the story of Cain and Abel present too advanced a picture of the civilization of primitive man (e.g., agriculture, etc.)?

Genealogies Genesis 5 and 11:10–32

2. How can these lists be genuine genealogies when the patriarchs are given such incredibly long lives?

The Flood Genesis 6:5–9:17

3. Compare the Biblical story of the flood with the flood narrative in the *Epic of Gilgamesh* and point out in detail both the similarities and the differences.

4. Was there really a flood which covered the entire earth?

The Tower of Babel Genesis 11:1–9

5. The tower of Babel resembles an actual type of tower which the Hebrews would have known and of which we have ruins today. Explain.

6. Did the tower of Babel incident really happen as it is described?

Religious Teaching

7. The religious teaching of all these incidents is what is important. Point out this teaching in each of the following and indicate how all together they form a pattern: (a) the Cain and Abel story; (b) the genealogies; (c) the flood story; (d) the tower of Babel story.

The Patriarchs (Genesis 12–50)

8. What type of history do we find in the story of the Patriarchs?

9. Why are God's promises to Abraham such an important part not only of his story but also of the Hebrew people?

10. Discuss the morality of the Patriarchs. It it consonant with our Christian code?

11. Show how their trials of faith were the central part of the lives of these Patriarchs.

12

THE HEBREW PROPHETS: AMOS

Readings: *Amos* 3, 4, 5 and the sections in the text.

References: *Prophets: Catholic Commentary:* 409a-418g; *G. Atlas:* pp. 90-92; *Sword:* chapter IX, pp. 150-168; *Guide:* Appendix IV. *Amos: Anderson:* pp. 228-237; *C. Commentary:* 524a-525; *Foreword:* pp. 76-78.

The Books

1. Explain the divisions of the prophetical books into the books of the former and latter prophets, the major and minor prophets.

The Prophets

2. What is the period of Hebrew prophecy and how do you explain that it has such fairly well-defined limits?

3. Give an exact definition of what is meant by Hebrew prophet and prophecy.

4. Examine *Exodus* 3, *Amos* 7:15, *Isaiah* 6 and *Jeremiah* 1:4–10 to see if they all contain a pattern that could be called the pattern of the prophetic call.

5. Do the prophetic "visions" mean that Yahweh always appeared physically to them, that when they say "the Lord says" they are always quoting God?

6. How were the people of Israel able to distinguish between the true prophets and their many false imitators? (Cf. *Jeremiah* 6:13–14; 28:1–9.)

Amos

Life

7. Give the date and historical background of the life of the prophet Amos.

Sins of Israel

8. Examine the following texts: 2:6–12; 4:1–5; 5:7, 10–26; 6:17, in which Amos condemns sins and social abuses to form a picture of the social and moral conditions of his day.

God

9. Explain from the texts the three qualities of the wrathful Yahweh presented by Amos: (a) 1–2; (b) 3:1–8; 4:6–11; 5:25–27; (c) 4:12–13; 5:8–9.

Punishment

10. The time of punishment (5:18ff.), its nature (6:8ff.), and the instrument of Yahweh's punishment (6:15) are shown in the texts cited. Explain.

11. What relationship is there between Amos' catalogue of abuses, his concept of Yahweh and Yahweh's punishment and the fact that he was originally a simple shepherd?

The Remnant

12. Against this somber background of sin and punishment, there is at least one ray of hope in 5:15; 9:9–15. Explain.

13

HOSEA

Date of events: 785–740 B.C.

Readings: Entire book.

References: *Anderson:* pp. 237-251; *C. Commentary:* 514a-514r; *Foreword:* pp. 74-75; *G. Atlas:* pp. 90-92.

The Book and the Man

1. When was the book written and what are its main divisions?

2. Who was the prophet Hosea?

The Times

3. What was the relationship between the Hebrews and Assyrians during Hosea's lifetime?

The Message

Hosea's Marriage

4. There are various interpretations of just what happened in Hosea's unhappy marriage. (Cf. 1:2–9 and 3:1–5.) Which do you prefer?

5. In any case, the symbolism of marriage is applied to Israel. How?

Israel and Yahweh

6. What does Hosea say in 4:1–19 about Israel's attitude towards Yahweh?

7. In 5:1–14 what does he say will happen to Israel?

8. Is Israel's repentance always genuine? (Cf. 5:15–6:4.)

9. What are some of Israel's continuing sins? (Cf. 6:5–7:16.)

10. What will be some of Israel's punishments? (Cf. 8–10:15; 11:12–13:19.)

11. Though Yahweh's love for Israel is spurned, how will it triumph? (Cf. 11:1–11.)

12. What is the great promise in chapter 14?

Summary

13. *Amos* and *Hosea* have many resemblances and many dissimilarities. Explain.

14

ISAIAH 1–39

Date of events: 740–700 B.C.

Readings: 1, 2, 6, 7, 8, 9, 11.

References: *Anderson:* chapter 9, pp. 252-287; *C. Commentary:* 419a-421e; *Foreword:* pp. 59-63; *G. Atlas:* 93-97; *Sword:* chapter X, pp. 169–188.

The Times

1. What is the historical background of this section of the Book of *Isaiah*?

The Man

2. Outline briefly the life and career of Isaiah.

3. Analyze his call in chapter 6.

4. How does Isaiah's withdrawal from public life help explain the composition of this section? (Cf. 8:9–18; 30:8–11.)

The Message

Monotheism

5. What is God's relation to the "nations" in *Isaiah*?

6. Does Isaiah's understanding of God's nature represent a major advance in Hebrew thinking about God?

7. What is meant by "holiness" in *Isaiah;* in the Old Testament; in our own times?

Morality

8. Explain the famous Song of the Vineyard in detail (5:1–7).

9. The "Day of Yahweh" is an extremely important element in the prophetic message of the Old Testament. It has already been seen in *Amos*. What advance is there in *Isaiah,* chapters 24–27?

Messianism

10. What is the occasion of the Emmanuel prophecy? (7:1–16).

11. In 7:14 does the Hebrew word necessarily mean Virgin? Relate this prophecy to Matthew 1:23.

12. What does *Isaiah* say about the coming (9:1–5) and the attributes (9:6–8) of the Messiah?

13. Explain the doctrine of the "Remnant" in *Isaiah*. (Cf. 10:20–22; 14:32; 18:7; and 37:33–35).

15

JEREMIAH

Date of events: 630-585 B.C.

Readings: 1-3, 7, 18-19, 26-28, 31, 36.

References: *Anderson:* pp. 297-305; chapter 11, pp. 325-356; *C. Commentary:* 452a-455e; *Foreword:* pp. 63–66.

The Book

1. Is there evidence in the book of *Jeremiah* itself that shows it is not chronologically or systematically arranged?

The Man

2. What are the three stages of the life of Jeremiah?

3. Analyze the call of Jeremiah (1:1–19) and compare it to that of Isaiah (6).

4. In *Jer.* 15:15–21 we see how absorbed Jeremiah is in his mission and how this makes him a type of Christ. Explain.

5. Explain Jeremiah's symbolic act in 18:1–17.

The Message: Monotheism

6. Show from 27:5–8 what the basis is for Israel's and Jeremiah's monotheism.

7. Analyze 11:1–14 to show the Covenant relationship between Yahweh and his people and its foundations in *Exodus* and the prophets before Jeremiah.

8. Show from 17:19–27 the intimate connection between belief in the one true God, the Law and the Day of Yahweh.

Morality

9. Israel's basic sin is described in 2:4–13. What is it?

10. Jeremiah also condemns social abuses in 22:13–17. What are they?

11. Show how in 31:27–30 he refines the Old Testament concept of collective guilt?

Messianism

12. What is messianic about 23:5–8?

13. The messianic prophecy of 33:14–22 raises an historical problem. What is its solution?

14. Analyze 31:31–34 to show the great importance of this passage and compare it with the *Epistle to the Hebrews* 8:7–12.

Summary

15. Compare and contrast Jeremiah with the other Hebrew prophets.

16

EZEKIEL

Date of events: 600–570 B.C.

Readings: 1, 4-5, 7, 20, 22, 23, 24, 27.

References: *Anderson:* chapter 12, pp. 357-375; *C. Commentary:* 477a-479e; *Foreword:* pp. 69-71; *G. Atlas:* pp. 98-99.

The Times

1. What critical events in Israel's history form the background of the book of *Ezekiel?*

2. In the religious development of the Hebrew people, why is this 50 year period of the Exile second only in importance to that of the Exodus?

The Man

3. Who was Ezekiel and where was he active as a prophet?

4. What do Ezekiel's visions (1; 37:1–14) and his strange, symbolic actions (2:8–3:4; 4:1–13; 5:1–10) reveal about his personality?

The Message

Monotheism

5. Explain Ezekiel's idea of God from chapters 1; 22; and 36:8–38.

6. Ezekiel's message is the boldest in language and imagery of all the prophetic writings. From 20:3–39 and 23:1–38 show how strikingly Ezekiel describes Israel's relationship to God.

Morality

7. What prophetic note is struck in chapter 7 and why?

8. Why do we find a reversal of this in 33:10–16; 33:21–22; 36:33–38; and 37:10–19?

9. What theme common to many of Israel's prophets do we find in chapter 22?

10. The Hebrews were only too ready to attribute their sufferings and their national tragedy to the sins of their ancestors. In chapter 18, how does Ezekiel shed new light on the complex problem of individual and collective responsibility?

Messianism

11. Compare the qualities of the new covenant in *Ezekiel* 36:22–32 with those of Jeremiah's in *Jer.* 31 especially 31:31–34 and show the importance of this concept for a correct understanding of both the Old and New Testament.

12. Explain Ezekiel's messianic teaching by examining his famous allegory in chapter 34:11–31, and his equally famous symbolic vision in chapter 37.

13. Ezekiel's messianism has sometimes been criticized as being too nationalistic and materialistic. Would you agree?

17

SECOND-ISAIAH 40-55

Date of events: 560-540 B.C.

Readings: 40-42; 49-53.

References: *Anderson:* chapter 13, pp. 394–429; C. Commentary 422a-f; *Foreword:* pp. 62-63.

The Book and the Man

1. What are the divisions of the book of *Isaiah?*

2. What is the basis of this division?

3. What do we know about the author of chapters 40–55, and what right do we have to call him Second-Isaiah?

4. What is the historical background of chapters 40–55?

The Message

Monotheism

5. W. F. Albright (*From the Stone Age to Christianity,* p. 327) says: "Deutero-Isaiah marks the culmination of the Mosaic movement . . . in his clear-cut and sweeping definition of the concept of ethical monotheism." Exemplify in *Is.* 40:12–31.

6. What is the book's attitude toward alien gods? How is this a more rational monotheism as compared to the practical monotheism of the Patriarchs? (Cf. *Is.* 41:1; 41:22–24; 41:28–29; 44:8–20; 45:22.)

7. The God of II Isaiah is a very different God from the terrifying God of *Exodus* and *Numbers.* Explain. (Cf. *Is.* 40:1–3; 40:10–11; 43:21; 51:15–16.)

Messianism

8. Analyze 40:1–11 in detail to show why Second-Isaiah can be called "the prophet of good news."

9. Show from 51:9–11 that Second-Isaiah's concept of redemption is that of a new Exodus and a new creation.

10. Read carefully the following "Servant Songs": 42:1–4; 49:1–6; 50:4–9; 52:13–53:12 and try to discover if for Second-Isaiah the Servant is Israel or an individual, or

both; and whether the Servant is a figure of the present or of the future, or both.

11. Though Second-Isaiah's message is a message of hope, it is a hope of things to be reached through suffering. Examine the "Servant Songs" for this idea and especially for the astonishing doctrine of the Servant's vicarious atoning.

12. Show from *Mark* 10:45; *Luke* 24:25–27; *Acts* 8:26–40; and *Philippians* 2:5-11 the great influence of this Servant theme on the New Testament.

13. Explain how chapters 54 and 55 act as a climax to the whole development of Second-Isaiah's thought.

18

DANIEL

Date of Book: 167-164 B.C.

Readings: 1-12.

References: *Anderson:* chapter 16, pp. 501-530; *C. Commentary:* 494a-495n; *Foreword:* pp. 72-74; *G. Atlas* pp. 102-110.

The Book and the Times

1. Have the discoveries of modern biblical scholarship forced us to revise our ideas about the author and date of composition of this book?

2. In the light of the above, explain more fully the historical background of the book.

The Literary Form

3. The literary form of the first six chapters is what the Hebrews called "haggadah." Explain.

4. The rest of the book is "apocalyptic" in form. Explain.

The Message

5. Outline briefly the stories in the first six chapters, pointing out the religious message of each.

6. By an analysis of the message in this section, some scholars have concluded that the author belonged to the Hasidim. Would you agree?

7. Describe and explain the vision in chap. 7, noting especially 7:13–14.

8. Have the apocalyptic visions of the book of *Daniel* influenced the New Testament in any way?

9. 7:13–14, is an important messianic text in *Daniel*. Compare this with 2:44; 4:14 and 9:15–27 and explain the messianic idea in *Daniel*.

10. It has been said that the message of *Daniel* on the after life (12:2-3) is due either to the influence of the Hellenistic milieu, the apocalyptic genre itself or simply to the attempt to create a theology of martyrdom. Is it any one or all of these? Explain.

19

MINOR HEBREW PROPHETS I

Readings: *Micah, Zephaniah, Nahum, Habakkuk, Lamentations, Baruch.*

References: *Anderson:* cf. Index references; *C. Commentary:* 533 (*Micah*); 541 (*Zephaniah*); 537 (*Nahum*); 539 (*Habakkuk*); 469 (*Lamentations*); 472 (Baruch); *Foreword:* pp. 66-69; 79-82.

1. Give the date and historical background, as well as some information on the authors of the following prophetic books: *Micah, Zephaniah, Nahum, Habakkuk, Lamentations, Baruch.*

Micah c. 730 B.C.

2. Like Amos and Hosea, Micah denounced the social injustices and sins of Israel. Give some examples and show how 6:1–8 is an admirable summary of his position.

3. Show how *Micah*, like *First Isaiah*, proclaims both punishment and restoration for Israel and how 4:7 and 5:2–6 are especially significant with regard to restoration.

Zephaniah c. 628–622 B.C.

4. Illustrate from the text the following judgment: "Into (Zephaniah's) conception of God's character, both justice and mercy enter; but the severe rather than the tender side of the divine nature is most accented."

5. Illustrate the following in the same way. "The religious value of the book (*Zephaniah*) lies in the profoundly earnest moral tone which pervades it."

Nahum c. 615 B.C.

6. It has been said that *Nahum* 2–3 represents some of the most vigorous poetry in Hebrew literature. Illustrate from the text the following critique: "The emotion animating it is tense and passionate; the language is singularly vigorous and dramatic, abounding in concrete and vivid imagery and containing scarcely a superfluous word."

7. The book of *Nahum* is unique among prophetical books in the attitude it takes toward Israel's morality. Explain by an analysis of the main ideas of the book.

Habakkuk c. 600 B.C.

8. The prophet Habakkuk alone amongst the prophets dares to call God to account for his government of the world. Analyze the dialogue in 1:2–2:4 to indicate the steps in the discussion between the prophet and Yahweh and compare 2:4 with the context of *Romans* 1:17, *Galatians* 3:11, and *Hebrews* 10:38.

9. What two aspects of Yahweh are presented through the lyric poetry of chapter 3?

Lamentations c. 575 B.C.

10. What is the *main* subject of the book of *Lamentations*? Give some examples from the text to show how aptly the Church uses this book to express our sorrow for Christ in his sufferings.

11. The book of *Baruch* contains a prayer of confession and hope in 1:15–3:8, a wisdom poem in 3:9–4:4 and a prophetical section in 4:5–5:9. Show from these texts how the religious life of the exiled Jews was kept alive in various ways.

20

MINOR HEBREW PROPHETS II

Readings: *Haggai, Obadiah, Jonah, Malachi, Joel, Zechariah.*

References: *Anderson:* cf. Index references; *C. Commentary:* 543 (*Haggai*); 530 (*Obadiah*); 531 (*Jonah*); 555 (*Malachi*); 522 (*Joel*); 545 (*Zechariah*); *Foreword:* pp. 75-76; 78-79; 83-85.

Historical Background

1. Give the date and historical background as well as some information on the authors of the following prophetic books: *Haggai, Obadiah, Jonah, Malachi, Joel, Zechariah.*

Haggai c. 520 B.C.

2. Show how the following judgment of *Haggai* is a mistaken one: "There is no longer a really spiritual message . . . the prophet seems to have included stones and timbers amongst the essentials of his spiritual and religious ideal."

Obadiah 5th century B.C.

3. Show how the brief book of *Obadiah* contrasts with the

universalism of Second Isaiah and yet presents a picture
of Yahweh consonant with Hebrew prophetic tradition.

Jonah 5th century B.C.

4. Many people know about Jonah and "the whale" but mis-
understand the meaning and significance of this section of
the book (chapter 2). Explain it correctly.

5. Show how not only the form of the book of *Jonah* differs
from that of the other prophets but also how its message,
at least in the great emphasis there given to it, is different
as well. Also explain how this makes Jonah a type of
Christ. (Cf. *Matthew* 12:39–42.)

Malachi c. 450 B.C.

6. Describe the sins of the Hebrew priests and people denounced by Malachi (1:6–2:9, 3:6–12) and show how according to him, the day of Yahweh will solve this problem
(3:1–5; 3:13–18).

7. Show the relationship between *Malachi* 3:1 and *Matthew*
11:10; *Luke* 7:27 and *Mark* 1:2; then point out the qualities of the Messianic era contained in *Malachi* 3:3–5
and 1:11.

Joel c. 400 B.C.

8. The Christian Church has found a great deal in the short
book of *Joel*. Show the relationship between Acts 2:16–21
and *Joel* 2:28–32, and then show why 1:13–20 and 2:12–27
are apt selections for the Church's Lenten liturgy.

9. Show the messianic implications of Joel 2:28–32 and the
importance of 3:2 and 3:12 for Christian thought about
the end of time.

Zechariah Chapters 1–8, c. 520 B.C.; chapters 9–14, end of 4th century B.C.

10. The principal religious teaching of the book of *Zechariah*
is messianic, but there is considerable difference between

the messianic teaching of chapters 1–8, and that of chapters 9–14. Illustrate from the text (a) how the messianic ideas in 1–8 are connected with the restoration of Jerusalem and the temple worship under Zerubbabel, and (b) how these ideas in 9–14 are connected with the figure of the new and everlasting Jerusalem, the universal kingdom of Yahweh, and the rejected shepherd. (Cf. *Matthew* 21:4; 26:31; 27:9; *John* 19:19–37.)

21

WISDOM LITERATURE

Date of books: *Proverbs* — final form 5th century B.C.
Qoheleth — 3rd century.
Wisdom of Solomon — 1st century.

Readings: Indicated in text.

References: *Anderson:* chapter 15, pp. 464-484; 498-500; *C. Commentary:* (*Proverbs*) 364a-365i; (*Qoheleth*) 376a-376o: (*Wisdom*) 388a-388l; *Documents:* pp. 270-278; *Foreword:* pp. 86-87; 94-98; 100-103; *G. Atlas:* pp. 102-111; *Sword:* chapters XII & XIV, pp. 211-226; 246-264.

The Writings of Wise Men

1. Explain the difference between "prudential" wisdom literature and "reflective" wisdom literature and give examples of each from both biblical and non-biblical ancient literatures, pointing out various similarities of both form and content.

2. "Reflective" wisdom literature in the Bible was written mainly in the post-exilic period and reflects its Hellenistic

milieu. The Hebrews reacted violently against their Greek
political rulers in the successful Maccabean revolt, but
since Hellenistic culture was the prevalent culture of the
Mediterranean world at this time, they were not able to
escape it in the same way. Examine the biblical "reflective"
wisdom literature to show how much of it is at once an
acceptance of Hellenistic culture and an apologetic against
it, based on the same unique religious insights that char-
acterize other parts of the Old Testament.

3. In the light of this influence of Hellenistic culture explain
   how the "wisdom" period of Hebrew history differs from
   the "prophetic" period.

Proverbs

4. The books of *Proverbs* contains only a few proverbs that
   are directly religious. Yet, the book is at bottom deeply
   religious. Discuss, for example, its attitude towards the
   direction of life by Yahweh (1:7; 3:5–12; 8:22–36; 16:1–11);
   towards one's neighbor (3:27–30; 6:1–5; 25:17; 26:18–19.)

5. In *Proverbs,* what is the attitude of the Hebrew wise
   man towards riches (22:4; 14:20 but also 8:10–11; 15:16);
   towards lending (11:15; 17:18 but also 19:17; 22:22–23);
   towards youth (13:24; 13:1); towards wine (23:20–21;
   23:29–32.)

Wisdom of Solomon

6. The book of the *Wisdom of Solomon* contains the high
   point of Hebrew thinking on the problem of life after
   death. Discuss its concept of immortality in chapter 2 and
   the connected discussion of the meaning of suffering in
   chapter 3.

7. The lengthy description of wisdom in the 7th chapter of
   the book of the *Wisdom of Solomon* presents it in an
   original way. What is the relationship of this concept with
   the New Testament revelation of the Trinity?

Song of Songs

8. Discuss the various meanings and interpretations of the *Song of Songs*.

Ben Sira

9. Discuss what *Ben Sira* says concerning wisdom and (a) the Law; (b) Temple worship; (c) moral conduct; (d) God. (Cf. Prologue; chapters 1–2; 51.)

Qoheleth

10. Qoheleth has been called "an unmitigated pessimist." Comment on this evaluation. (Cf. chapters 1–3; 9; 12.)

22

JOB

Date of book: around 495.

Readings: 1-14; 38-42.

References: *Anderson:* pp. 484-497; *C. Commentary:* 317a-319h; *Foreword;* pp. 87-90; *Sword:* chapter XIII, pp. 227-245.

The Book

1. When was the book written?

2. Was the author a Hebrew?

3. Into what category of biblical books does *Job* fall? Explain.

4. Give an outline of the major divisions of the book.

The Problem

5. What is the problem of the book of *Job* as posed in the prologue, chapter 1?

6. This problem springs from a conflict among Hebrew re-

ligious beliefs in (a) the deuteronomic theme; (b) Sheol; (c) the justice and faithfulness of Yahweh. Explain.

Job's Friends

7. What solution do Job's friends have to offer to the problem?

8. What is Job's answer to their well-meant but unsatisfactory attempts to console him?

9. Is there much progression of ideas in the dialogue between Job and his friends?

10. What does Elihu add when he intervenes?

11. What is Job's reaction to this apparently fruitless search for a solution?

12. Does 19:25–27 mean that Job had faith in resurrection after death? What does "redeemer" mean here?

Yahweh in the Whirlwind

13. What solution to the problem is offered by Yahweh in chapters 38–41?

14. What is Job's reaction to this solution in 42:1–6?

The Epilogue

15. In the light of all the above, does the Epilogue really fit into the scheme of the book, or does internal evidence indicate that it may have been a later addition?

23

THE PSALMS

Date of Psalms: From the 10th to the 4th centuries.

Readings: In text below.

References: *Anderson:* pp. 444-445; *C. Commentary:* 334-339h and sections dealing with individual *Psalms* cited below; *Documents:* pp. 151-154; *Foreword:* pp. 91-94.

1. What does the word Psalm mean?
2. How many *Psalms* are there? Why is it that they are numbered differently in the various versions?
3. Is David the author of the *Psalms*?
4. What are some of the characteristics of Hebrew poetry?
5. What important part have the *Psalms* played in the history of the Church?

The book of the *Psalms* is one of the most comprehensive expressions of Israel's religion found in the Old Testament. Rather than trying to determine the message of the *Psalms*, we shall examine the literary forms found in the book. The Psalms listed below were selected as typical examples of the more important subdivisions of the four important literary forms to be found in the *Psalms*. Be prepared to discuss each one in some detail, e.g.:

(a) What is the theme of this *Psalm*?
(b) How is it constructed?
(c) What does it say about God, Man, Sin, the Messiah?

A. HYMN   PSALM
  6. Cosmic   8
  7. Historical   113

B. PRAYERS

  8. Collective   60
  9. Collective   85
 10. Individual   22
 11. Penitential   50

C. DIDACTIC

D. PROPHETIC AND ESCHATOLOGICAL

24

FINAL SURVEY I

Interpretation of Scripture

1. Implied in the basic principle of Scriptural interpretation, "the meaning of any written document can be discovered only by searching for what the author intended to say," are the following questions: (a) who is the author of Scripture? (b) what role does man play in its composition? (c) how was our present Old Testament text assembled? (d) why is recognition of various literary forms so important for understanding its message?

Hebrew History

2. Abraham's call and journey, the Exodus, the invasion of Palestine, the reigns of Saul, David and Solomon, the division of the Kingdom, the fall of the Northern and Southern Kingdoms, the Exile, the return from Exile, the periods of Persian and Greek domination, the Maccabean revolt and Hasmonean rule are all cardinal events in Hebrew history. Give the approximate date of each event,

and explain the political and military relationship of the Hebrews to the power dominant in the Fertile Crescent at the time. Comment also on the uniqueness of the Hebrew idea of history.

The Covenant

3. The Covenant relationship between Yahweh and Israel is absolutely basic. Describe how the events of Exodus are the foundation for it; show the Hebrews' particular understanding of miracles; then go into some detail on the meaning of Covenant and its promulgation on Sinai. Finally, point out some significant renewals of the Covenant in Hebrew history and some important references to it in some of the later books.

The King

4. Kingship in Israel is also important from a religious point of view. Explain first the soul-searching that the nation went through before it chose a king, then show how David was considered the perfect king because of his religious contributions, how the Deuteronomic historian says the Kingship failed, and finally explain how in the prophets the Messiah becomes a king-figure and the messianic era his kingdom.

Creation

5. The great creation epic in *Genesis* is a good example of how Israel was influenced by contemporary literary and cultural currents and yet managed to preserve its own unique religious point of view. Explain this by discussing such points as creation itself, the creation of man and of woman, paradise, the fall, and the flood.

25

FINAL SURVEY II

The Person of God in Prophetic Literature

1. Show how the various prophets emphasized different aspects of the person of Yahweh, pointing out as well how the political and cultural conditions through which the nation passed influenced their thinking on this subject.

Idolatry

2. Though the idols took various forms and shapes, Israel's greatest temptation, before the exile at least, was idolatry, that is, the worship of something or someone besides Yahweh. Show from the prophets how they were tempted to deify the gods of the Canaanites, their own prosperity, the might and wealth of Babylon, Assyria and Persia, as well as the culture of Greece, then give the means that the prophets used in attempting to turn them from these various idolatries.

The Messiah

3. The messianic idea in Israel was a complex one: partly political and military, partly religious. Explain both of these aspects in general, then show how the various prophets brought out the religious aspect of the Messiah, though perhaps in different ways.

The Problem of Suffering

4. When they were a young nation, the Hebrews found a solution to the problem of suffering that seemed to them satisfactory. As time went on, however, they began to have their doubts about the complete validity of this solution,

doubts which were epitomized in the book of *Job*. Later on, they heard but did not at the time fully understand *Second-Isaiah*'s mystical solution. Finally, through a new understanding of individual responsibility in the prophets and a reëvaluation of the after-life as seen in *Daniel* and *Wisdom*, they arrived at a final solution, one which prepared the way for the revelation of the New Testament. Explain each of these steps.

Wisdom

5. Explain, by a brief examination of each, how the books of *Proverbs, Wisdom, Ben Sira,* and *Qoheleth* were both an assimilation of Gentile culture and an apologetic against it.

PART 3

Appendices

APPENDIX I

Egyptian and Accadian Creation Texts, and the Epic of Gilgamesh[1]

EGYPTIAN CREATION TEXT (Carved in 6th Dynasty pyramid—24th cent. B.C. ANET p. 3)

O Atum-Kheprer (2 phases of sun—later Atum-Re), thou wast on high in the primeval hill (symbolized by the pyramid); thou didst arise as the ben-bird of the ben-stone in the ben-house in Heliopolis; thou didst spit out what was Shu (god of air), thou didst sputter on what was Tefnut (goddess of moisture) . . . O Great Ennead which is in Heliopolis, Atum, Shu, Tefnut, Geb (god of earth), Nut (goddess of sky), Osiris, Isis, Seth, and Nephthys, whom Atum begot, spreading wide his heart in joy at his begetting you . . .
(Also other creation texts, repulse of dragon, etc.)

"Enuma Elish" ("When on high") *ACCADIAN CREATION EPIC* (early 2nd millennium)

When on high the heaven had not been named
Firm ground had not been called by name,
Naught but primordial Apsu, their begetter,
And *Mummu-Tiamat*,[2] she who bore them all,
Their waters commingling as a single body:

---

[1] Parentheses and emphasis added to the *Creation Texts* by the Editor of the Study Guide.

Parentheses and emphasis added to the *Gilgamesh Epic* by the Translator.

[2] "Mummu" means "mother." "Tiamat" is "the sea," etymologically akin to "tehom," i.e. "the deep" in Gen. 1:2.

No reed hut had been matted, no marsh land had appeared,
When no gods whatever had been bought into being,
Uncalled by name, their destinies undertermined—
Then it was that the gods were formed within them . . .
        (ANET p. 60-61: Tab. I, lines 1-9)

(Gods are named, including Marduk and Ea)
(Eventually, Tiamat "prepared for battle against the gods, her
offspring"; Tab. II, line 2)

Then joined issue Tiamat and Marduk, wisest of gods.
They strove in single battle, locked in combat . . .
He released the arrow, it tore her belly,
It cut through her insides, splitting the heart.
Having thus subdued her, he extinguished her life . . .
The lord trod upon the legs of Tiamat.
With his unsparing mace he crushed her skull . . .
Then the lord paused to view her dead body,
That he might divide the *monster* and do *artful works.*
He split her like a shellfish into two parts:
Half of her he set up and *ceiled it as sky,*
Pulled down the bar and posted guards.
He bade them to allow not her *waters to escape.*
He crossed the heavens and surveyed the regions.
He squared Apsu's quarter, the abode of Nidimmud,
As the lord measured the dimensions of Apsu.
The Great Abode, its likeness, he fixed as Esharra,
The Great Abode, Esharra, which he made as the *firmament.*
Anu, Enlil, and Ea he made to occupy their places. (ANET
        pp. 66-67: Tab. IV, lines 93-146)

Tablet V:

He constructed stations for the great gods,
Fixing their *astral likenesses* as *constellations.*
He determined the year by designating the zones:
He set up three constellations for each of the twelve months.
After defining the days of the year by means of heavenly
        figures,

He founded the station of Nebiru (planet Jupiter) to determine their heavenly bands,
That none might transgress or fall short . . . etc. (ANET p.
67: Tab. V, lines 1-7 . . .)

In her (Tiamat's) belly he established the zenith.
The *Moon* he caused to shine, the night to him appointing.
Thou shalt have luminous horns to signify six days,
On the seventh day reaching a half-crown.
At full moon stand in opposition in mid-month.
When the sun overtakes thee at the base of heaven,
Diminish thy crown and retrogress in light . . .", etc. (ANET
p. 68: Tab. V, lines 11-20)

Tablet VI (Creation of *man*)

When Marduk hears the words of the gods,
His heart prompts him to fashion artful works.
Opening his mouth, he addresses Ea
To impart the plan he has conceived in his heart:
"Blood I will mass and cause *bones* to be.
I will establish a savage, *"man"* shall be his name.
Verily savage-man I will create.
He shall be charged with the *service of the gods* that they
might be at ease! . . ."
Ea answered him, speaking a word to him,
Giving him another plan for relief of the gods:
"Let but one of their brothers be handed over:
He alone shall perish that mankind may be fashioned . . ."
(The Assembly judges the god Kingu guilty of having incited
Tiamat to revolt)
They bound him (Kingu), holding him before Ea.
They imposed upon him his guilt and severed his blood
vessels.
Out of his *blood* they fashioned *mankind.*
He (Ea) imposed the *service* and let *free* the gods.
After Ea, the wise, had created mankind,
He imposed upon it the service of the gods . . ." (ANET p. 68:
Tab. VI, lines 1-35)

(Next, the lesser gods construct a great *Tower of Babylon* "as high as Apsu" (sky), in which "the 50 great gods took their seats")

GILGAMESH EPIC (c. 2000 B.C.) *Tree of Life* (Flood story just precedes this)

(Utnapishtim the Faraway says to Gilgamesh) "I will disclose, O Gilgamesh, a hidden thing, and a secret of the gods I will tell thee:

This *plant,* like the buckthorn is

Its thorns will prick thy hand just as does the rose.

If thy hands obtain the plant, thou wilt find *new life*."

No sooner had Gilgamesh heard this

Than he opened the water-pipe (he is in a boat, by the way, —he pulled the plug)

He tied heavy stones to his feet.

They pulled him down into the deep and he saw the plant.

He took the plant, though it pricked his hands.

He cut the heavy stones from his feet.

The sea cast him up upon its shore.

Gilgamesh says to him, to Urshanabi, the boatman:

"Urshanabi, this plant is a plant apart,

Whereby a man may regain his *life's breath*.

I will take it to ramparted Uruk (G's home town)

Will cause . . . to eat the plant . . . ! (text corrupted here)

Its name shall be '*Man Becomes Young in Old Age*.'

I myself shall eat it and thus return to the state of my *youth*."

After twenty leagues they broke off a morsel,

After thirty further leagues they prepared for the night.

Gilgamesh saw a well whose water was cool.

He went down into it to bathe in the water.

A *serpent* snuffed the fragrance of the plant;

It came up from the water and *carried off the plant* . . .

Thereupon Gilgamesh sits down and weeps

His tears running down over his face. (ANET p. 96: Tab. XI, lines 266-291)

GILGAMESH EPIC cont'd *Flood Story* (ANET pp. 93-95:
  Tab. XI, lines 13-183)

That city was ancient—(as were) the gods within it,
When their heart let the great gods to produce the flood.
(*There*) *were* Anu, their father, . . .
Valiant Enlil, their counselor,
Ninigiku-Ea was also present with them;
Their words he repeats to the reed-hut:
"Reed-hut, reed-hut! Wall, Wall!
Reed-hut, harken! Wall, reflect!
Man of Shuruppak, son of Ubar-Tutu,
Tear down (this) house, build a ship!
Give up possessions, seek thou life.
Forswear (worldly) goods and keep the soul alive!
Aboard the ship take thou the seed of all living things.
The ship that thou shalt build,
Her dimensions shall be to measure.
Equal shall be her width and her length.
Like the Apsu thou shall ceil her."
I understood, and I said to Ea, my lord:
"Behold, my lord, what thou has thus ordered,
I will be honored to carry out.
(But what) shall I answer the city, the people and elders?"
Ea opened his mouth to speak,
Saying to me, his servant:
"Thou shalt then thus speak unto them:
'I have learned that Enlil is hostile to me,
So that I cannot reside in your city,
Not set my f(oo)t in Enlil's territory.
To the Deep I will therefore go down, to dwell with my
    lord Ea.
(But upon) you he will shower down abundance,
(The *choicest*) birds, the *rarest* fishes.
(*The land shall have its fill*) of harvest riches.
(He who at dusk orders) the husk-greens,
Will shower down upon you a rain of wheat.' "

With the first glow of dawn,
The land was gathered (about me). (too fragmentary for
    translation)
The little ones (carr)ied bitumen,
While the grown ones brought (all else) that was needful.
On the fifth day I laid her framework.
One (whole) acre was her floor space, ten dozen cubits the
    height of each of her walls,
Ten dozen cubits each edge of the square deck.
I laid out the contours (and) joined her together.
I provided her with six decks,
Dividing her (thus) into seven parts.
Her floor plan I divided into nine parts.
I hammered water-plugs into her.
I saw to the punting-poles and laid in supplies.
Six "sar" (measures) of bitumen I poured into the furnace,
Three sar of asphalt (I also) poured inside.
Three sar of oil the basket-bearers carried,
Aside from the one sar of oil which the *calking* consumed,
And the two sar of oil (which) the boatman stowed away.
Bullocks I slaughtered for the (people),
And I killed sheep every day.
Must, red wine, oil, and white wine
(I gave the) workmen (to drink), as though river water,
That they might feast as on New Year's Day.
I op(ened) . . . ointment, applying (it) to my hand.
(On the sev)enth (day) the ship was completed.
(*The launching*) was very difficult,
So that they had to shift the floor planks above and below,
(*Until*) two-thirds of (*the structure*) (*had g*)one (*into the*
    water).

(Whatever I had) I laded upon her:
Whatever I had of silver I laded upon her;
Whatever I (had) of gold I laded upon her;
Whatever I had of all the living beings I (laded) upon her.
All my family and kin I made go aboard the ship.

The beasts of the field, the wild creatures of the field, all the
    craftsmen I made go aboard. . . .

Consternation over Adad reaches to the heavens,
Who turned to blackness all that had been light.
(The wide) land was shattered like (a pot)!
For one day the south-storm (blew),
Gathering speed as it blew, (submerging the mountains),
Overtaking the (people) like a battle.
No one can see his fellow,
Nor can the people be recognized from heaven.
The gods were frightened by the deluge,
And, shrinking back, they ascended to the heaven of Anu.
The gods cowered like dogs crouched against the outer wall.
Ishtar cried out like a woman in travail,
The sweet-voiced mistress of the (gods) moans aloud: . . .

Six days and (six) nights
Blows the flood wind, as the south-storm sweeps the land.
When the seventh day arrived, the flood(-carrying) south-storm
    subsided in the battle,
Which it had fought like an army.
The sea grew quiet, the tempest was still, the flood ceased.
I looked at the weather: stillness had set in,
And all of mankind had returned to clay.
The landscape was as level as a flat roof.
I opened a hatch, and light fell upon my face.
Bowing low, I sat and wept,
Tears running down on my face.
I looked about for coast lines in the expanse of the sea:
In each of fourteen (regions) there emerged a region (-moun-
    tain).
On Mount Nisir the ship came to a halt.
Mount Nisir held the ship fast, allowing no motion. . . .

When the seventh day arrived,
I sent forth and set free a dove.
The dove went forth, but came back;

Since no resting-place for it was visible, she turned round.

Then I sent forth and set free a swallow.

The swallow went forth, but came back:

Since no resting-place for it was visible, she turned round.

Then I sent forth and set free a raven.

The raven went forth and, seeing that the waters had diminished,

He eats, circles, caws, and turns not round.

Then I let out (all) to the four winds and offered a sacrifice.

I poured out a libation on the top of the mountain.

Seven and seven cult-vessels I set up,

Upon their pot-stands I heaped cane, cedarwood, and myrtle.

The gods smelled the savor,

The gods smelled the sweet savor,

The gods crowded like flies about the sacrificer. . . .

When at length as Enlil arrived, and saw the ship, Enlil was wroth,

He was filled with wrath over the Igigi gods: "Has some living soul escaped?

No man was to survive the destruction!" . . . "Instead of thy bringing on the deluge,

Would that a lion had risen up to diminish mankind! . . ."

APPENDIX II

Some Principles to Help Toward the Understanding of Genesis 1-11

A. *Discern the general purpose of the narrative.* This purpose is didactic, theological. What these chapters wish to convey are the historical events and the theological facts that form the foundation of the religion of the one true God. These events and facts are known ultimately by God's revelation of them. The narrative details (e.g. the talking serpent) belong to the method of presenting the doctrine. The people of that time had no way of checking on the historicity (in our modern sense) of these details, and attached no independent importance to them, and hence, had *no intention of affirming their historicity*. These chapters are intent on *affirming the truth of the doctrine* which touches the relation of mankind to God. Since this doctrine is linked to the dimension of time, we may say that these chapters deal with history, but not history in our modern sense of the word with all its passion for scientific accuracy in chronology and geography. History for them was not primarily the relation of man with man but man with God. These chapters therefore affirm the creation of all things by God at the beginning of time, His special action in creating man, man's original state of elevation, man's rebellion and fall, God's promise of future salvation, how sin multiplied in the hearts of men, etc.

B. *Distinguish between the substance and the literary form of the narrative.* As far as the literary form or dress or

method of presentation is concerned, remember that the
writer (or writers) sometimes used popular stories from
Mesopotamia as a means of more effectively putting over
his religious teaching, e.g., Tower of Babel. "When an
Israelite related history he moralized, and when he moralized, he told a story."—Grollenberg, "Atlas of the Bible"
—p. 27 (Read the full essay on p. 27.)

C. *Recognize the peculiar characteristics of these ancient
literary forms.* Here are some aspects that help us to determine the type and the extent of the author's affirmation
about the details of the narrative:

1. Use of the primitive, naïve and popular notions about
   the universe;
2. Anachronistic portraiture: after the Fall of Man, Adam,
   Cain, Abel and others are described in terms of a much
   later culture;
3. Meshing of several and sometimes disparate traditions
   without bothering about the apparent inconsistencies,
   e.g., the Flood story;
4. Recasting of popular Mesopotamian stories from a
   strictly monotheistic standpoint, with a view to better
   inculcating a religious truth, e.g., Flood, Babel;
5. Cultural rather than physical genealogy: the Table of
   Nations in *Genesis* 10.

D. *Learn the specific purposes of the narrative in Genesis 11-1.*

1. Serves as a majestic prologue to the narrative of the
   Patriarchs in *Genesis* 12ff.
2. Teaches God's attitude to sin most effectively.
3. Teaches the fundamental truths of Yahwism. The theological teaching, which is uppermost in the mind of the
   author, is very advanced.
4. Illustrates the so-called process of selectivity or elimi-
   nation by which the author concentrates his attention,
   chiefly through genealogies, on the characters who will
   be the ancestors of the Chosen People: Adam, Seth,

Lamech, Noe, Sem, Thare. World history thus becomes, gradually, Israel's history.

5. Has a polemic purpose, against the gross polytheism of Israel's neighbors, which is easily discernible.

E. *A few words of advice on reading, studying, and talking about these chapters:*

1. *Stress the certainties:* doctrinal truths about God, creation, nature and elevation of man, original sin, fall, God's holiness, mercy . . .

2. *Avoid confusing* such certainties with probabilities and those things about which we are at present ignorant (e.g., "giants" in 6/4).

3. Enter the mind of the oriental narrator and appreciate his literary forms. The artificial character of *Genesis* 1, for example, clothes a tremendously important doctrinal affirmation: God's part in the origin of the world.

4. Admit there are many secondary problems still unsolved: e.g., longevity in *Genesis*.

APPENDIX III

Some Differences Between the Ancient Hebrew Historian and the Modern Scientific Historian

Ancient Hebrew Historian

Sources: Chiefly Oral Tradition (Stories)
Some Written Material

He tries to reconstruct the past as the collective memory of his people remember it. When memory fails, the imagination is used.

Oral tradition has a tenacity for detail, yet allows variation, i.e., transference of an episode from one individual to another; from one setting or time to another setting or time.

He reports the core, the substance of the event.

He has no sense of chronology. He will often read his own cultural setting back into the past.

He presents several versions of one event; he uses parallel narratives. This is why substantially the same stories are told more than once with change of characters and setting.

Modern Scientific Historian

Sources: Documents (Written records)
Monumental Remains

He tries to reconstruct the past objectively and exactly.

He relies upon what is written, therefore what is fixed and permanent.

He tries to give a complete and accurate report of an event.

He carefully reconstructs the chronology.

From all his material he reconstructs only one account of an event.

He evaluates material, using elementary logic, common sense.	He is highly critical of his sources. He applies the principles of historical method.
He does not guarantee the veracity and accuracy of every statement.	He vouches for the veracity and accuracy of every statement.
He writes "history" with a unique emphasis: to teach a religious truth, to instill a religious conviction.	He tries to write history without undue emphasis. His purpose is to try to recount the past.

The history that we read in the Old Testament is historical. In their own way the Ancient Hebrew historians report real events. They give us a faithful picture of the origins and social, moral and religious actions of the People of Israel.

The history of the Old Testament is substantially accurate, although the imagination is used when the collective memory fails.

In the Old Testament we do not look for history in the modern sense of the word. What then are we to call that type of narrative which we find in the Old Testament? We accept the common description of history as "the remembered past" and we accept the fact that the remembered past is recorded, both among uncivilized peoples as well as civilized peoples, when the scientific historian is not at work, in the "STORY."

In the "STORY" the past is not remembered for its own sake but for some personal, social or some other special reason. The remembrance is conditioned by the capacity of the oral traditions (the stories) to retain what happened. The storyteller, taking the material from oral tradition, does not merely recount the past; he tries to recreate it. He demands the right to give a free and, to some degree, an imaginative account. His listeners are willing to grant him this.

An Introduction to the Prophets

THE NAME. The Old Testament name for prophet is 'nabi'. The original meaning of this word seems to be 'to announce, to call out.' The 'nabi' then would be someone who calls out or announces, both of which meanings bring us close to the heart of Israelite prophetism. The prophet thus is a messenger and interpreter of the divine word. The modern notion then of a prophet as a 'foreseer of the future' falls short of the mark.

IRRESISTIBLE CALL. This divine word that comes to them is irresistible, they cannot stop it, 'Comes the divine warning, who will but prophesy.' Amos 3:8. Jeremiah puts up a vain fight against it, Jer 20:7-10. In Amos 7:15, Is 6, and Jer 1:4-10, we see how they were chosen as God's messengers and how much this cost them. For it meant that not only their words but their whole lives were to be 'signs' of God's will. Their lives thus become a prophecy. Cf. Hos 1-3; Is 20:3, 8:18; Jer 16; Ezek 4:3.

HOW MESSAGE RECEIVED AND TRANSMITTED. The divine message can come to the prophet in a variety of ways. It can come as a vision as in Is 6 or Ezek 1,2,8; it can come as a dream as in Num 12:6, Deut 7; it can come as something heard; but most of the time it comes by interior inspiration. This last is what the standard formulas mean: 'The word of Yahweh came to me . . . the word of Yahweh. . . .' Once this message was received it could be transmitted by the prophet in any number of forms, as a lyrical poem, passage of prose, parable or narrative, an oracle, stylized curses, diatribe, wisdom writing, cultic psalm, love song, satire, or elegy.

MYSTICAL INSTRUMENT.   Though this variety in the reception and transmission of the message depends in large part on the temperament of the individual prophet, there is one trait that is characteristic of every real prophet: they are all aware that they are instruments, that their words are theirs yet not really theirs. This conviction is based on a mysterious experience, a contact with God which we can call mystical. If, as in the cases of the great mystics, this sometimes produces some external signs of strangeness, this is only secondary and accidental. This contact with God places the prophet on a 'supra-normal' psychological level. It is a supernatural state quite different from that of poetic inspiration.

TYPE OF MESSAGE.   The prophet's message is concerned with the present and the future. Though he speaks to his contemporaries, warning them of punishment for faults and reward for conversion, his message can be above time. But his 'predictions' are only to confirm his 'preaching.' The more recent prophets look all the way to the last days in order to draw a message for the present. Since it is God's message, it can surpass even the prophet's consciousness and remain immersed in mystery until the future makes it clear as with the Messianic prophecies.

TRUE AND FALSE PROPHETS.   Due to his mystical experience the prophet is personally sure that he speaks in Yahweh's name. But how can the people distinguish the true prophets from the false which appear fairly frequently in the Bible? Whether sincere or deluded, they look enough like true prophets that these latter have to campaign against them. According to the Bible, there are two ways of identifying a true prophet: 1) the fulfillment of the prophecy, Jer 28:9; and 2) the conformity of their teaching with Yahwistic doctrine. Cf. the norms of the Church for 'private' revelations.

SUMMARY.   The prophet is a man who has experienced God directly, who has received the revelation of his holiness and his wishes, who judges the present and sees the future in the light of God, and who is sent by God to remind men of his demands and to bring them back to the ways of obedience and love.

THE DOCTRINE OF THE PROPHETS: A SYNTHESIS

MONOTHEISM: Monotheism is nothing new for the prophets. They but recall the ancient truths and build their warnings and teachings upon them. However, the full meaning and implications of monotheism become clearer in them. At Sinai the one true God was revealed as Israel's own God. The prophets recall this but they also show that he is the God of other nations as well. Thus he gives and takes away the power of other states, guides them, uses them as instruments of his vengeance. Cf. Amos 9:7; Amos 1-2; Jer 27:5-8; Is 7:18-19. They even go so far as to predict that though the temple is Yahweh's dwelling place it will be destroyed. Mic 3:12; Jer 7:12-14.

As the one true God He could leave no place to other gods, as is affirmed throughout the Bible. During the Exile when the temptations of syncretism became strongest, the polemic against idols is stepped up by the prophets, but it now becomes more rational. Is 40:19-20; 41:6-7, 21-24; 44:9.20. The triumph of monotheism is also emphasized by them. Is 44:6-8; 46:1-7-9.

This unique God is 'holy,' that is transcendent. Cf. Is 6, 1:4; 5:19, 24; 10:17-20. Also Hos 11:9; Is 40:25, Jer 50:29. As Ezekiel emphasizes, Ezek 1, he is surrounded by mystery, infinitely above the 'sons of men,' and yet he is close by his goodness, the tenderness which he shows to his people. Cf. the allegory of marriage between Yahweh and Israel in Hos 2 and Jer 2:2-7; 3:6-8.

MORALITY: The opposition of man's impurity to God's sanctity, that is, the sense of sin, is not new with the prophets, but they do have an intense awareness of it. They underscore the fact that it is sin which separates man from God,

Is 59:2. For Amos, sin is a blow at the God of Justice, for Hosea, at the God of Love, for Isaiah, at the God of Sanctity. For Jeremiah, sin is at the center of his vision, extending out to the whole nation which appears to be irretrievably corrupt. Jer 13:23. It is this superabundance of evil which calls down the great punishment of God, the terrifying 'day' of Yahweh. Is 2:6-22; 5:18-20; Hos 5:9-14. Though they frequently speak in terms of collective sin and punishment, the notion of individual responsibility appears in Jer 31:29-30 and especially Ezek 18. The positive answer to sin, a good life, deepens correspondingly. One must seek God, carry out his commands, live in humility, have an interior religion. Amos 5:4; Is 1:17; Hos 10:12; Mic 6:8; Jer 31:31-34. It is this spirit which must vivify the whole liturgical cult of Yahweh, to avoid a ritualism empty of all moral significance. Is 1:11-17; Jer 6:20.

MESSIANISM: Punishment is never Yahweh's last word. Despite all their apostasies, the Israelites are still yearning for the accomplishment of the promises, and Yahweh remains faithful to them. He will spare a 'Remnant.' Amos 5:15; Is 4:3ff. These are the ones who at once escape present danger and attain final salvation. After each trial, the Remnant is the group that has survived, Amos 5:15; Jer 24:8; Zech 8:6, 11, 12. But this group is also the germ of a holy people to whom the future is promised. Is 11:10. This future will be a time of unheard-of happiness, though these perspectives of material power are secondary to the spiritual accomplishment of the kingdom of God with its spirit of holiness, justice, pardon, and happiness. To establish this kingdom, Yahweh will 'anoint' a representative, that is the Messiah. He is for Isaiah 'God with us,' Is 7:14, and for Jeremiah 'Yahweh is our justice.' This great hope survived the most incredible catastrophes, including the Exile. Then, however, the Messiah is presented as a mediator or pastor, Zech 9:9, and especially as the servant of Yahweh in Is 42:1-7; 49:1-9; 50:4-9 and especially 52:13-53:12. In Daniel he comes on a cloud and receives

dominion over all peoples. These references remained mysterious. In applying them to Christ, the New Testament makes
them speak with infinitely more meaning than they did to
their first hearers.

APPENDIX V

The Chronological Background of the Old Testament

BEFORE HEBREW MEMORY

Origin of *universe:* In the order of 3-5 (or 7?) billion years ago.
Origin of *man:* c. 1 million or 200,000 B.C.

STONE AGE It began at least 100,000 B.C.

1) *Paleolithic:* ended with retreat of last glacier. c. 10,000-8,000 B.C.
2) *Mesolithic:* transitional stage between food-gathering and food-producing. c. 8,000-5,500 B.C.
3) *Neolithic:* first villages and first use of pottery. c. 5,500-4,000 B.C.

CHALCOLITHIC AGE c. 4,000-3,300 B.C.

Copper introduced. Writing began in Mesopotamia (c. 3500 B.C.)

BRONZE AGE c. 3,300-1,000 B.C.

1) *Early Bronze:* c. 3,000-2,000 B.C.
First great Dynasties and Empires arise in Mesopotamia and Egypt.
2) *Middle Bronze:* c. 2,000-1,500 B.C.
ABRAHAM appears in Ur (C. 1900 B.C.). HEBREW MEMORY BEGINS.

WITHIN HEBREW MEMORY	O.T. BOOKS
PATRIARCHAL AGE (c. 1900-1700 B.C.) Abraham, Isaac, Jacob in Palestine Joseph, migration to Egypt (c. 1700 B.C.)	GENESIS 12-50
EXODUS (c. 1290-1220 B.C.) Oppression by Pharaoh c. 1290: Departure under Moses; Mt. Sinai: Law, Covenant c. 1291-1250: Wanderings in desert c. 1250: Journey between Edom and Moab through Sihon to Mt. Nebo	EXODUS NUMBERS
JOSHUA-CONQUEST OF PALESTINE (c. 1250-1225 B.C.) c. 1250 or 1230: Fall of Jericho Up to c. 1225: Capture of much of Canaan	JOSHUA
PERIOD OF THE JUDGES (c. 1225-1020 B.C.) 1) c. 1200: Invasion of coastal plain by Philistines 2) c. 1100-1020: Battles with Philistines 3) c. 1050-1020: SAMUEL-last Judge, anoints *KINGS*	JUDGES 1 SAM 1-10
UNITED KINGDOM (1020-922 B.C.) 1) *Saul* (1020-1004): First King, anointed by Samuel, slain 2) *David* (1000-961): Defeat of Philistines, Jerusalem becomes capital 3) *Solomon* (961-922): Built first Temple, material apogee of Kingdom	1 SAM 10-31 2 SAM 1 KG 1 1 KINGS 2-11

DIVIDED KINGDOM (922-721-587 B.C.)
1) Israel (North): (922-721): 19 Kings
  a) 721: *Assyrian* conquest of Israel, Samaritans transplanted there
2) Judah (South): (922-587); 20 Kings
  a) 597: *Babylonian* conquest of Judah— first stage of *Exile*
  b) 587: Destruction of Jerusalem and Temple—second stage of *Exile*
3) Classical Prophets begin to appear in the 8th century
	1 KINGS 12-22
	
	2 KINGS

BABYLONIAN EXILE (597 & 587-538 B.C.) 1) Activity of *Prophets* during the exile, especially II Isaiah 2) 539: *Cyrus* conquers Babylon and establishes *PERSIAN* Empire 3) Decree of Cyrus, ending Babylonian Exile	2 KINGS 25:27-30 2 CHR 36:22-23
PERSIAN PERIOD (538-333 B.C.) 1) Rebuilding of city walls and second Temple 2) Activities of Zerubbabel, Ezra, Nehemiah	EZRA NEHEMIAH

HELLENISTIC PERIOD (333-167 B.C.)
1) 333: *Alexander* conquers Persia
2) 323: Death of Alexander—his empire broken into three pieces, controlled by Egypt, Syria, Greece
3) *Status of Palestine*
  a) 323-198: Under Egypt—distant, tolerant control
  b) 198-167: Under Syria (Selucids)—attempt to impose pagan Hellenism
  c) 167: Profanation of Temple by Antiochus IV—Maccabean revolt	

MACCABEAN KINGDOM (165-63 B.C.) 1) 167-165: Revolt under leadership of the Maccabees 2) 165-63: Independent Jewish Kingdom (8 Kings) 3) 134: Death of Simon Maccabeus—*End of Old Testament Chronology*	1 and 2 MACCABEES
ROMAN PERIOD 1) Begins in 63 B.C. with conquest of Palestine by Pompey	

Glossary

AB: The name of the fifth month of the Babylonian and Jewish calendar. It corresponded, approximately, to our month of August.

ADAR: The twelfth month of the Jewish year. The name was borrowed from the Babylonian calendar during the Exile.

ACHAEMENIAN: The name given to the Persian Empire of Cyrus the Great and his successors. The word is derived from Achaemenes, a Persian king of the seventh century, who gave his name to the whole Achaemenian Dynasty.

ALLEGORY: It is a literary form consisting of an extended comparison which is used to teach a moral or religious lesson. The comparison is based upon an extended series of metaphors, each with its appropriate meaning. Isaiah made use of allegory in chap. 5:1-7, comparing, by a sustained metaphor, Israel to a carefully tended vine. A Parable is also a comparison but, unlike the Allegory, each detail is not meant to have a particular application.

AMARNA AGE: That period in Egyptian history dominated by the Pharaoh Akh-en-Aton (1377-1360). At his capital, Tell el-Amarna, more than 350 letters were found, written on clay tablets. These letters were sent from Syria, Palestine, and Mesopotamia, to the Egyptian court. The tablets, discovered in 1887, are of great historical value for the light they shed on the Near East of that period.

APOCALYPTIC LITERATURE: A form of writing which consists in describing divine revelations usually given to some famous biblical character of the past (Adam, Noah, Henoch, etc.). These revelations, which always look to the future, are communicated in mysterious and symbolic language. Apocalyptic writing is later than Prophetic literature, and is especially popular in a time of crisis. Much of *Daniel* is apocalyptic.

APOCRYPHA: The Books, or parts of books, of the Old Testament, which were handed down in Greek, and were denied the rank of Holy Scripture in the Jewish Canon of Scripture. Protestants follow this Canon. Among Catholics these Books are called "Deuterocanonical." The Council of Trent, in 1546, declared these Writings to be sacred and canonical. The books which Catholics call "Apocrypha" are not inspired and therefore not in the Bible.

APOLOGETICS: The systematic defense, through the light of natural reason, of the teachings of the Catholic Church.

ARAMAIC: A Semitic language which, as early as the eighth century B.C., became the international language of commerce and politics in the Near East. In Palestine it succeeded in replacing Hebrew as a living language. Our Lord and the Apostles spoke Aramaic.

ARCHAEOLOGY: The science which studies the life and culture of man as it is revealed through excavation. Biblical Archaeology is concerned with every discovery which can throw light on the biblical record.

BAAL: The king of the gods and the leader of the Canaanite pantheon. He was a storm-god and a giver of fertility. The word *ba'lu* means "lord, master."

BIBLICAL COMMISSION: Established by Pope Leo XIII in 1902, its membership is made up of Cardinals, assisted by Consultors from all parts of the world. Its duties are to direct and control the teaching of Sacred Scripture throughout the Catholic world. The Commission also has the right to confer academic degrees in Sacred Scripture.

CANON: The authoritative collection of sacred writings, recognized and received as inspired by the Catholic Church. The Catholic Canon of Scripture was solemnly defined in 1546 at the Council of Trent.

CARCHEMISH: A settlement located on the modern frontier between Turkey and Syria, at the western bend of the Euphrates. It was the site of one of the decisive battles of history (605 B.C.). The victory of Babylon over Egypt set the stage for the Babylonian Captivity of the Jews.

CODEX: An ancient book, made up of separate leaves fastened together. In antiquity it competed with, and finally supplanted, the payrus roll, which was made by glueing papyrus sheets so as to form one long strip. In biblical times the roll was the common writing material (See *Luke* 4:16-20).

UNCIAL CODEX: An ancient manuscript written in capital letters. These manuscripts are ordinarily of superior legibility and beauty. The "minuscule" is the opposite of the "uncial." The most important uncial codices of the Bible are:

A. *Codex Sinaiticus,* from the fourth century A.D., containing Old and New Testaments. Formerly at St. Catherine's Monastery on Mt. Sinai it is now in the possession of the British Museum.

B. *Codex Vaticanus,* from the fourth century A.D., with both Old and New Testaments. It is the property of the Vatican Library.

C. *Codex Alexandrinus,* from the fifth century A.D., with both Old and New Testaments. It is now in the British Museum.

All three of these codices are written on sheets of vellum, prepared from the skins of animals. They are written in Greek.

COVENANT: An agreement between two or more persons. In the Old Testament the word refers to the bond between Yahweh and Israel, which is the basis of Israel's religion. Christ came to establish a New Covenant which He sealed with His death on the Cross.

DAY OF YAHWEH: A great day of judgment in which the wicked will be punished, and holiness and peace will triumph. It is an eschatological (end of time) term. In the New Testament it is the Day on which Christ, as Judge, will come in the glory of the Father.

DEUTEROCANONICAL: The sacred books of either Old or New Testament about whose divine origin there had been some doubts. See CANON.

EXEGESIS: The science of correctly interpreting the text of the Bible. It comes from a Greek word meaning "to explain."

FEAST OF PURIM: It was instituted to celebrate the deliverance of the Jews from their mortal enemy, Haman. He had cast a "pur" (lot) to determine the day of the massacre of the Jews. The Feast is kept in the middle of the Jewish month of Adar, which ordinarily coïncides with our month of February.

FEAST OF TABERNACLES: It is also called the "Feast of Booths." The Feast is kept in the autumn, at the end of the agricultural year. The booths, set up during the Feast, remind the Jewish people of the Exodus and their wanderings in the wilderness.

FEAST OF WEEKS: Sometimes it is called the "Feast of the Harvest." It is celebrated fifty days after Passover, and thus corresponds to the Christian Pentecost.

HANUKKAH: The Feast which celebrates the Purification and Rededication of the Temple by Judas Maccabeus. This took place in 165 B.C. The Hebrew word *hanukkah* means "dedication." The Feast is celebrated in the Jewish month of Chislev, which corresponds approximately with our December.

HASMONEAN HOUSE: Commonly used to designate the ruling family of the Maccabean Age, from Mattathias to Herod the Great. The family name of Mattathias was probably "Hashmonay."

HELLENISM: The pursuit of Greek culture and the cultivation of the Greek language by people who were non-Greeks.

The Hellenistic Rule in the Near East extends from the victory of Alexander the Great at the Battle of Issus (333 B.C.) to the Conquest of Palestine by Pompey (63 B.C.).

HIGHER CRITICISM: The study of the Bible from a literary and historical viewpoint. It is to be distinguished from Lower (textual) Criticism which aims to reproduce, as far as possible, the text as it came from the original author.

INERRANCY: That quality of Sacred Scripture by which the assertions of its authors are free of all error. Inerrancy is a necessary consequence of inspiration.

INSPIRATION: The supernatural impulse by which God has moved the human author to write in such a way that God is the principal author. The human writer is an instrumental cause, but also a true author.

LEVIRATE LAW: If a man died childless, the Mosaic Law obliged the brother of the deceased to marry the widow. In this way children were raised up in the name of the first man, and the dead man's name did not perish in Israel. (*Deut.* 25:5ff.)

MARCION: He was a heretic of the second century who rejected the entire Old Testament and parts of the New Testament, in his canon of Sacred Scripture.

MARI: An ancient city on the banks of the Middle Euphrates, discovered in 1933 and excavated by French archaeologists. The City flourished in the time of Hammurabi (1728-1686). The royal archives, consisting of over twenty thousand tablets, are now in the process of publication.

MER-NE-PTAH: He was Pharaoh of Egypt in the Imperial Era. He set up the famous "Israel Stele" on which he inscribed his Hymn of Victory, about 1220 B.C. The Stele is important for determining the time when Israel entered the land of Canaan.

NIPPUR: A sacred City of the Sumerians, and a religious center of the god En-lil, "Lord of the Storm." The valuable Sumerian literature found at the site is now in the Museums of Istanbul and the University of Pennsylvania.

NUZU: An ancient site in eastern Mesopotamia, near modern Kirkuk, Iraq. Since the first excavations in 1925, numerous tablets from this mound have been published, giving us a better understanding of the Patriarchal Age.

PAPYRUS: A tall plant which flourishes along the marshes of the Nile. It was used extensively as writing material in the ancient world. Many papyrus texts have been preserved for centuries in Egypt because of the dry climate which prevails.

PARABLE: A popular story told to illustrate a moral or religious truth. Parables formed an important part of our Lord's teaching. The parables of the Good Shepherd, the Unjust Steward, and the Good Samaritan, may be cited as examples. See ALLEGORY.

PARALLELISM: This is a characteristic quality of Hebrew and other Semitic poetry. It consists in balancing the two equal parts of a single verse. The second half of the verse may express the same idea as the first half (synonymous parallelism), or the exact opposite (antithetic parallelism). Examples of this stylistic quality abound in the *Psalms* and *Proverbs*.

PASSOVER: This is the most solemn Jewish festival of the year; it celebrates their deliverance from Egypt, as narrated in *Exodus*. The festival begins on the 14th of Nisan (usually in the month of April) with the eating of the Paschal Lamb, and continues for seven days. The Passion of our Lord took place during the Feast of the Passover (Pasch) in Jerusalem.

PHARISEE: The word is derived from Hebrew and means "to separate." The Pharisee was a member of a religious party which probably originated at the time that Hellenism threatened Judaism in Palestine. The religious life of a Pharisee centered in the Law and its interpretation. The danger of excessive legalism was always present.

POST-EXILIC: The Babylonian Exile, 587-538, marked a turning-point in the history of Israel. Events, institutions, and writings which belong to the period after the Return to Palestine in 538, are called "post-Exilic."

RAMSES II: (1290-1224) This Pharaoh of the Nineteenth Dynasty was famous for the massive monuments with which he covered Egypt. Biblical tradition connects the oppression of the Israelites with the building of two of his cities in the Nile Delta, Pithom and Ramses.

RAS SHAMRA: See "UGARIT."

REDACTION: A redactor is one who prepares or edits literary material for publication. The finished product is a redaction. In a redaction we sometimes find rearrangement, revision, or adaptation of the original material.

SADDUCEES: A Jewish religious party which was recruited largely from the priestly and aristocratic class. The Pharisees, on the contrary, drew largely from the mass of the populace. Both parties, though opposed to one another on specific points of theology, appear together in the New Testament as adversaries of our Lord.

SAPIENTIAL LITERATURE: These are writings which sought to study the nature of things and their relation to man and God. Though much of this literature was the product of observation and experience, wisdom was nevertheless a gift of God and was given only to the man who feared God. Sapiential is derived from the Latin word "sapiens," meaning "wise."

SATRAPY: A title used during the Persian period to denote a province under the control and protection of the King of Persia. The authorized representative of the king was called a "satrap" or "protector" of the land.

SELEUCID: This name was given to the succession of Syrian kings who controlled Jerusalem from 198 B.C. until the time of the Maccabean struggle in 165 B.C. The founder of the Dynasty was Seleucus I, who established Seleucid rule over Syria, Mesopotamia, Persia, and the southern part of Asia Minor. The Dynasty was Hellenistic in its culture.

SEPTUAGINT: This Greek work is the best known and most important translation of the Old Testament. The word "Septuagint" means "seventy," and recalls the legend that seventy men composed the board of translators. The Septuagint translation was practically complete by the end of the second century B.C.

SHEOL: According to Old Testament ideas of the future life Sheol was the place where the spirits of the dead continued to exist. It was a place below the earth, shadowy and depressing. Another name for it was "the Pit."

STELE: (or "stela") is a Greek word denoting an erect stone slab which is used for a memorial inscription. The tombstone is a very common example of the Stele. In ancient times, victories were often recorded on a stele.

SUMER: The ancient name for the southern part of Babylonia. It was the site of the earliest civilization in the Near East. The chief cities of Sumer were Nippur, Lagash and Ur.

THEOPHANY: A manifestation or appearance of God to man. This could be either in person, as at Sinai, or by means of the Angel of the Lord.

TYPOLOGY: The science of determining the typical sense in the Old Testament. God, the principal author of Scripture, has intended that certain persons, institutions or things should signify and point ahead to some person, institution or thing in the New Testament. The Paschal Lamb is a type of Christ, as the Manna is a type of the Holy Eucharist.

UGARIT: This ancient Canaanite city on the eastern shore of the Mediterranean is more commonly known as Ras Shamra (fennel head). Discovered in 1928, excavations were begun the following year by a French archaeological expedition and are still in progress. The most important find at Ras Shamra has been the ancient Canaanite literature which has greatly aided our understanding of many biblical passages.

VULGATE: This is St. Jerome's Latin version of the Bible, completed in 405 A.D. It derives its name from the Latin word *vulgare* "to publish, make common, spread abroad." The translation, a landmark of Christian latinity, became the official

Bible of the Church in the West, and was the first book to be printed on the Gutenberg Press.

WELLHAUSEN: Julius Wellhausen (1844-1918) was a German biblical scholar and orientalist. He is best known for his defense and popularization of the Documentary Hypothesis as applied to the first six books of the Bible. His false theological and historical suppositions have rendered many of his conclusions obsolete.

ZION: The southeast hill of Jerusalem which was captured by David from the native Jebusites and renamed the "City of David." Zion is sometimes used in the Old Testament to signify all of Jerusalem. It may also denote that spiritual Jerusalem which is a symbol of the true Church.

APPENDIX VII

Variant Spellings of
Old Testament Books

Study Guide	Confraternity—Douay Knox	Abbrev.
Genesis		Gen
Exodus		Exod
Leviticus		Lev
Numbers		Num
Deuteronomy		Deut
Joshua	Josue	Josh
Judges		Jdg
Ruth		Ruth
1 Samuel	1 Kings	1 Sam
2 Samuel	2 Kings	2 Sam
1 Kings	3 Kings	1 Kgs
2 Kings	4 Kings	2 Kgs
1 Chronicles	1 Paralipomena	1 Chr
2 Chronicles	2 Paralipomena	2 Chr
Ezra	1 Esdras	Ezra
Nehemiah	2 Esdras or Nehemias	Neh
Tobit	Tobias	Tob
Judith		Jth
Esther		Est
Job		Job
Psalms		Ps
Proverbs		Prov
Qoheleth	Ecclesiastes	Qoh
The Song of Songs		Cant
Wisdom of Solomon	Wisdom	Wis
Ben Sira	Ecclesiasticus	Sir
Isaiah	Isaias	Is
Jeremiah	Jeremias	Jer

Study Guide	Confraternity—Douay Knox	Abbrev.
Lamentations		Lam
Baruch		Bar
Ezekiel	Ezechiel	Ezek
Daniel		Dan
Hosea	Osee	Hos
Joel		Joel
Amos		Amos
Obadiah	Abdias	Obad
Jonah	Jonas	Jon
Micah	Michaeas	Mic
Nahum		Nah
Habakkuk	Habacuc	Hab
Zephaniah	Sophonias	Zeph
Haggai	Aggaeus	Hag
Zechariah	Zecharias	Zech
Malachi	Malachias	Mal
1 Maccabees	1 Machabees	1 Mac
2 Maccabees	2 Machabees	2 Mac

APPENDIX VIII

Guide to Pronunciation

ACHAEMENIAN
(ah-kay-méan-ian)
ADAR (ah-dár)
AHASUERUS (a-ha-zoo-ér-us)
AHAZ (áy-haz)
AKH-EN-ATON (ack-en-áh-ton)
AMALEKITES (ah-mál-eh-kites)
AMEN-EM-OPET
(amen-em-óh-pet)
ANATOTH (án-a-toth)
ANTIOCHUS (antíe-o-cuss)
ASAPH (áy-saf)
ATHALIAH (ath-ah-ly'e-ah)
BAAL (báy-al)
BALAAM (báy-lam)
BALAC (báy-lak)
BARUCH (bár-uk)
BETHULIA (beth-óo-lee-ah)
BOAZ (bóh-as)
CANAAN (káy-nan)
CARCHEMISH (kár-kay-mish)
CHEBAR (káy-bar)
DEPHKAH (déf-kah)
DEUTERONOMY
(due-ter-ón-oh-me)
DIASPORA (die-áss-po-rah)
ECCLESIASTES
(e-klee-zee-áss-teez)
ECCLESIASTICUS
(e-klee-zee-áss-ti-kuss)
EDOM (ée-dum)
ELEAZAR (el-ee-áy-zar)

ELIHU (eh-ly'e-hue)
ELIJAH (ee-ly'e-jah)
ELIMELECH (eh-li'm-e-leck)
EPHRAIM (éf-rah-im)
EPIPHANES (eh-píf-fah-neez)
ESDRAELON (ez-dra-áy-lon)
EXODUS (ék-so-duss)
EZEKIEL (e-zéek-ee-el)
EZION-GEBER
(áy-zee-on géb-er)
GENESIS (jén-e-sis)
GENIZAH (ge-née-zah)
GIDEON (gíd-ee-un)
GILBOA (gil-bó-ah)
GLUECK (glick)
HABAKKUK (háb-ah-cook)
HAGGAI (hág-eye)
HAMAN (háy-man)
HAMMURABI
(ham-moo-ráh-bee)
HANUKKAH (hah-núk-kah)
HASMONEAN (haz-mo-née-an)
HOSEA (hoe-záy-ah)
HYKSOS (hík-sauce)
ISAIAH (eye-záy-ah)
JEHOIACHIN (jeh-hóy-ah-kin)
JEREMIAH (jer-eh-my'-ah)
JEROBOAM (jer-oh-bó-am)
JOSHUA (jósh-you-ah)
JOSIAH (joe-cy'-ah)
LACHISH (láy-kish)
LEVITICUS (leh-vít-i-cuss)

203

MACCABEES (máck-ah-bees)
MALACHI (mál-ah-ky)
MARI (máh-ree)
MASHAL (mah-shál)
MEGIDDO (meg-gi'd-doe)
MER-NE-PTAH (mare-nép-tah)
MERODACH (meh-róe-dak)
MICAH (my'-kah)
MORDECAI (mór-de-kai)
NAHUM (náy-hum)
NAOMI (nay-óh-mee)
NEBUCHADNEZZAR
 (ne-byu-khad-néz-zar)
NEHEMIAH (nee-he-my'-ah)
NICANOR (nee-káy-nor)
NIPPUR (níp-poor)
NUZU (nóo-zoo)
OBADIAH (oh-ba-díe-ah)
PARALIPOMENON
 (pa-ra-li-póm-en-on)
PENTATEUCH (pén-tah-tyuk)
PHARAOH (fáir-oh)
POMPEY (póm-pee)
QOHELETH (ko-hél-eth)
RAHAB (ráy-hab)
RAMSES (rám-sees)
SAMARIA (sah-máre-ee-ah)
SATRAPY (sáy-trap-ee)
SEIR (sáy-ir)

SELEUCID (se-lóo-sid)
SENNACHERIB (sen-nák-er-ib)
SEPHER TEHILLIM
 (sáy-fer teh-hil-léem)
SEPTUAGINT (sép-tu-ah-jint)
SERABIT EL-KHADEM
 (sér-ah-bit el-káh-dem)
SHEAR YASHUB
 (shée-ar-yáh-shoob)
SHEOL (shé-ole)
SHEPHELAH (sheh-fáy-lah)
SHISHAK (shy'-shak)
SIRACH (sére-ak)
STELE (stéel-ee)
SUMER (sóo-mer)
TELL ABIB (tell-ah-béeb)
TIGLATH PILESER
 (tíg-lath pie-lée-zer)
UGARIT (yóu-gah-rit)
UZZIAH (uz-zy'e-ah)
XERXES (zérk-sees)
YAHWEH (yáh-way)
ZECHARIAH (zek-ah-ry'e-ah)
ZEDEKIAH (zed-eh-ky'e-ah)
ZEPHANIAH (zef-an-éye-ah)
ZERUBBABEL
 (zer-óob-bah-bell)
ZION (zái-on)

APPENDIX IX

Maps

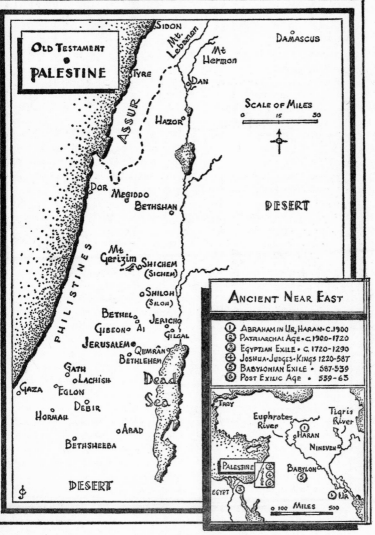

OLD TESTAMENT PALESTINE

SIDON
Mt. Lebanon
Mt Hermon
DAMASCUS
TYRE
DAN
ASSUR
HAZOR

SCALE OF MILES
0   15   50

DOR
MEGIDDO
BETHSHAN

DESERT

Mt Gerizim
SHICHEM (SICHEM)
SHILOH (SILOH)
BETHEL
GIBEON   Ai
JERICHO
GILGAL
JERUSALEM
QUMRÂN
BETHLEHEM
GATH
LACHISH
GAZA
EGLON
DEBIR
HORMAH
ARAD
Dead Sea
BETHSHEEBA

PHILISTINES

DESERT

ANCIENT NEAR EAST

① ABRAHAM IN UR, HARAN - C. 1900
② PATRIARCHAL AGE - C. 1900-1720
③ EGYPTIAN EXILE - C. 1720-1290
④ JOSHUA-JUDGES-KINGS 1220-587
⑤ BABYLONIAN EXILE - 587-539
⑥ POST EXILIC AGE - 539-65

TROY
Euphrates River
Tigris River
HARAN
NINEVEH
PALESTINE
BABYLON
EGYPT
UR

0 100   MILES   500

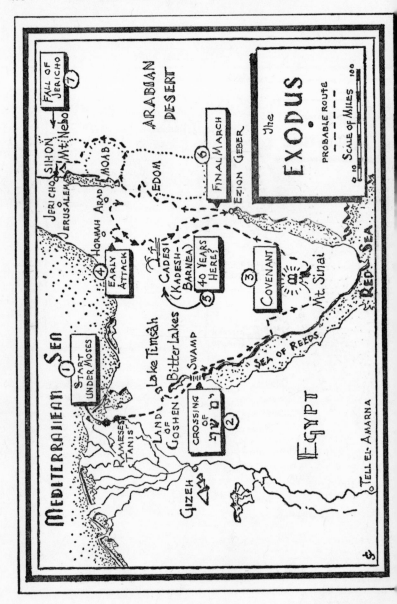

APPENDIX X

Bibliography

*ALBRIGHT, WILLIAM F.
From the Stone Age to Christianity
Doubleday (Anchor), New York, 1957

*ALBRIGHT, WILLIAM F.
Archaeology and the Religion of Israel
Johns Hopkins Press, Baltimore, 1946

*ALBRIGHT, WILLIAM F.
Archaeology of Palestine
Penguin Book, Baltimore, 1949

*ANDERSON, BERNHARD W.
Understanding the Old Testament (Anderson)
Prentice-Hall, New Jersey, 1958

*BRIGHT, JOHN
A History of Israel
The Westminster Press, Baltimore, 1959

CHARLIER, DOM CELESTIN
The Christian Approach to the Bible
Newman, Westminster, 1959

DANIEL-ROPS, HENRI
Sacred History
Longmans, Green & Company, New York, 1949

DOUGHERTY, JOHN J.
Searching the Scriptures
Hanover House, Garden City, 1959

---

* Asterisk indicates non-Catholic works.

NOTE: The parenthesis following the title of some of the books in the bibliography indicates the code word used for it in the reference sections of the text.

*GLUECK, NELSON
   The Other Side of the Jordan
   American Schools of Oriental Research, New Haven, 1940

*GOTTWALD, NORMAN K.
   A Light to the Nations: An Introduction to the Old Testament
   Harper, New York, 1959

GROLLENBERG, L. H., O.P.
   Atlas of the Bible (G. Atlas)
   Nelson, London, 1956

GROLLENBERG, L. H., O.P.
   Shorter Biblical Atlas
   Nelson, New York, 1959

HAURET, CHARLES
   Beginnings: Genesis and Modern Science
   Priory Press, Dubuque, 1955

HEINISCH, PAUL (trans. HEIDT, WILLIAM G., O.S.B.)
   A History of the Old Testament
   Liturgical Press, Collegeville, Minnesota, 1952

JONES, ALEXANDER
   Unless Some Man Show Me
   Sheed and Ward, New York, 1951

*KENYON, KATHLEEN M.
   Archaeology in the Holy Land
   Frederick A. Praegh, New York, 1960

*KENYON, KATHLEEN M.
   Digging up Jericho
   Ernest Benn, Ltd., London, 1957

MCKENZIE, JOHN L., S.J.
   The Two-Edged Sword (Sword)
   Bruce Publishing Co., Milwaukee, 1956

MORIARTY, FREDERICK L., S.J.
   Foreword to the Old Testament (Foreword)
   Weston College Press, Weston, 1954

MORIARTY, FREDERICK L., S.J.
   Introducing the Old Testament
   Bruce Publishing Co., Milwaukee, 1960

MURPHY, ROLAND E. O. Carm.
   Seven Books of Wisdom
   Bruce Publishing Co., Milwaukee, 1960

ORCHARD, DOM BERNARD (ED.)
A Catholic Commentary on Holy Scripture (C. Commentary)
Nelson, New York, 1953

*PRITCHARD, JAMES (ED.)
The Ancient Near East in Pictures Relating to the Old Testament
Princeton University Press, New Jersey, 1954

*PRITCHARD, JAMES (ED.)
Ancient Near Eastern Texts Relating to the Old Testament, 2nd
    ed. (ANET)
Princeton University Press, New Jersey, 1950, 1955

ROBERT, A., and TRICOT, J. (Trans. ARBEZ, E. T. and MCGUIRE, M.)
Guide to the Bible, 2nd ed., Vol. I
Desclee, New York, 1960

*THOMAS, D. WINTON
Documents from Old Testament Times (Documents)
Nelson, New York, 1958

VAWTER, BRUCE C. M.
God's Story of Creation (Creation)
Knights of Columbus Pamphlet

*WRIGHT, GEORGE ERNEST, and FILSON, FLOYD V.
The Westminster Historical Atlas to the Bible, rev. ed. (W. Atlas)
SCM Press Ltd., London, 1957